Banner Designs
for
Celebrating
Christians

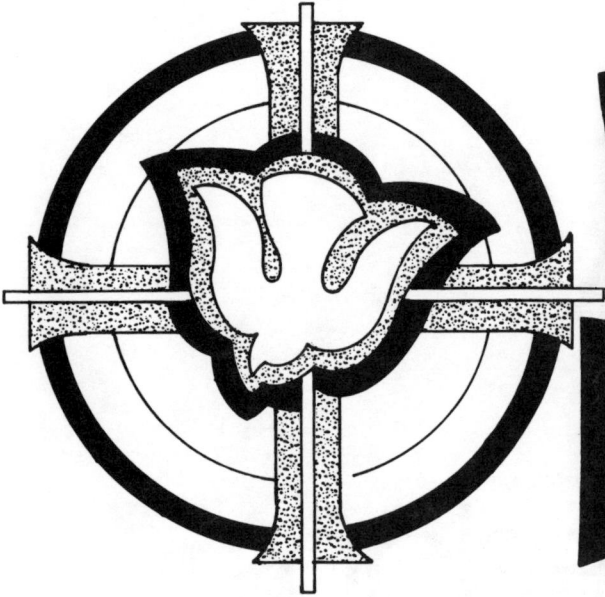

Banner Designs For Celebrating Christians

by Jane DeBord
and Linda Isbell

Publishing House
St. Louis

Copyright © 1984 Concordia Publishing House
3558 S. Jefferson Avenue, St. Louis, MO 63118-3968
Manufactured in the United States of America

Library of Congress Cataloging in Publication Data

DeBord, Jane, 1943-
    Banner designs for celebrating Christians.

      1. Church pennants. I. Isabell, Linda, 1950-
II. Title.
TT850.2.D43 1984   746.9   83-23191
ISBN 0-570-03930-4

     4 5 6 7 8 9 10   SB   93 92 91 90 89 88

CONTENTS

KNOW YOUR TEXTURES AND COLORS

Colors can visually express emotion. For example, red, yellow, and their derivatives reflect joy and high moments, whereas the cooler tones of blue and its variations suggest contemplation or tranquility. The use of colors will determine the emphasis of each banner. For instance, using complementary colors against each other produces a striking, jump-out-at-you effect, while using similar colors will result in a more subdued effect. For illustration, put a piece of bright yellow fabric against a piece of dark purple fabric—note the contrast. (A complementary color chart is on the following page.)

A graduation of progressive tones of similar colors (for example: yellow, orange, orange-red, red) produces an effect of increasing intensity. This technique works well when a powerful effect is desired.

Textures reflect moods in the same manner as colors. For example, marriage is a festive occasion calling for the finest of fabrics. A funeral, on the other hand, combines grief and celebration. The banner reflects this through a combination of rough and high sheen textures.

The seasons of Lent and Advent call for some rough-textured fabrics, symbolizing in Lent the agony and suffering of our Lord and in Advent His humble birth in a crude manger. High sheen fabrics are suitable for most other seasons and occasions.

Chart of Complementary Colors

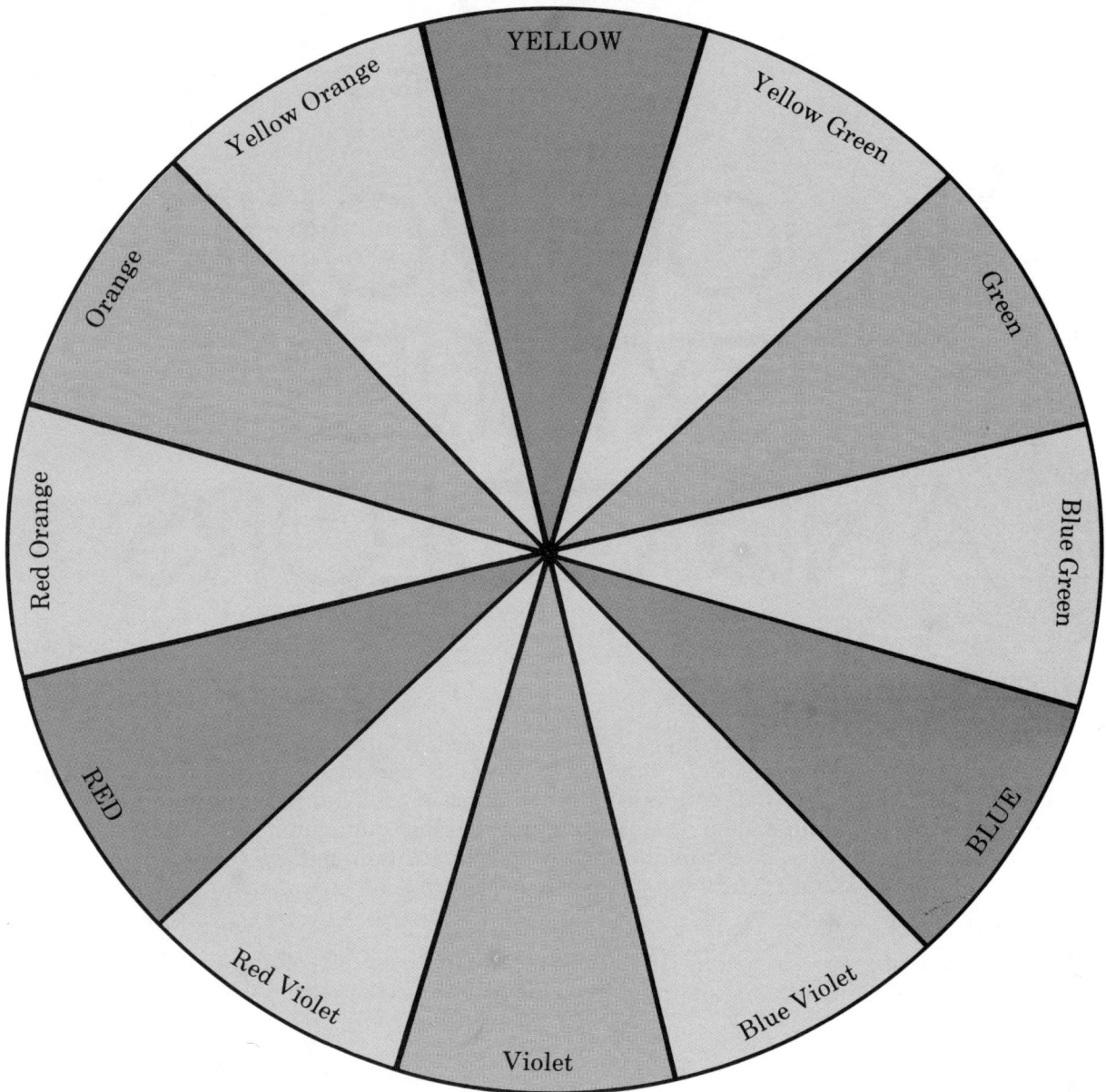

YELLOW

Yellow Orange

Yellow Green

Orange

Green

Red Orange

Blue Green

RED

BLUE

Red Violet

Blue Violet

Violet

PLACE AND PURPOSE OF BANNER

Before you choose a location for your banner, remember that placement will determine the size and will also influence the potential effect of the banner. If the chosen setting is a formal sanctuary, keep in mind the mood or atmosphere that already exists—the architecture, stained glass, crosses, and the colors of existing paraments, carpeting, and curtains.

Look around your church. There are probably many bare walls that could use a face-lift from a colorful banner. Use banners wherever they can accomplish their purpose.

A banner not only can enhance the beauty of its surroundings, but it can also motivate, inspire, and call forth responses of action or thought. A banner can be the perfect solution to the problem of calling attention to a specific concern of the church (examples: stewardship campaign, upcoming revival, World Communion Sunday). Let your banner work for you!

SCALE TO SIZE

Every banner design in this book can be easily scaled to a size suitable for your particular space. All methods involve using roll art paper or butcher paper, which comes in a variety of widths. If a wide roll is not available to get a large enough sheet on which to draw the banner pattern, simply tape two smaller pieces together. Three methods can be used to obtain the required banner size:

1. If an opaque projector is available, enlarge the design in the book to the desired size and trace it.

2. If an opaque projector is unavailable, enlarge the banner design according to a scale. Each design is measured in inches (for example: 3″ x 5 ½″). The scale for enlarging the design is to have one inch represent one foot (1″ = 1′—a 3″ x 5 ½″ design becomes a 3′ x 5 ½′ banner). Draw a grid on the chosen banner design with horizontal lines across at every inch and vertical lines up and down at every inch. Draw the outside perimeter of the finished banner size (for example: 3′ x 5 ½′) on the roll art paper. Draw a grid on the paper at every foot in the same manner. The lines of the banner design in the book will cross the grid at certain points. These points should be marked on the design and then transferred to the large pattern at the corresponding points. Lines are then drawn to connect the points by copying the curve or angle from the design in the book. The design may vary slightly from the original but should be similar enough to accomplish the intended purpose.

3. If the space where the banner will hang does not allow you to enlarge it according to the scale of 1″ = 1′, or if you choose to make the banner larger than the intended scale, you can create your own scale. (For example a 1″ = 1 ½′ scale will mean that a 3″ x 5 ½″ design will make a 4 ½′ x 8 ¼′ banner. A 1″ = ½′ scale will produce a 1 ½′ x 2 ¾′ banner). The same system of drawing grids on the design and the pattern, transferring the points, and drawing the approximate lines can then be used.

CONSTRUCTION

1. Draw the banner pattern to scale. Keep this pattern in one piece to use as a background for the placement of individual pieces.

2. Trace the individual pieces of the pattern. Be certain before this step is done that you have studied the banner to see if any part of a particular piece is covered by another piece. (For example, the words "Wonderful, Counselor" in the Advent banner, "He Shall Be Called . . .," cover part of the starburst in the background.) The entire piece must be traced, including lines that are covered by another part of the banner.

3. Decide how much fabric is needed for each part of the banner. Purchase the fabric, lining (same yardage as for the background piece), thread, fusible interfacing on both sides (Stitch Witchery), and rods at a fabric store. For the background piece purchase six inches more than the finished banner size to allow for top and bottom finishing. If thin or light fabric will be covering dark fabric at any spot, you will need to use double fabric and Stitch Witchery so that the darker fabric will not show through.

4. Number the pattern pieces in the order in which they will be placed on the background, layer by layer. (For example, on the "He Shall Be Called . . ." banner the starburst would be #1, and the letters that go on top of the starburst would be #2.)

5. Cut the background. Be sure you have left at least six inches to finish off the top and bottom of the banner.

6. Cut the pattern pieces. Lay out Stitch Witchery on the bottom, then the fabric, and then the pattern piece on top. Pin all three pieces together. Cut the pieces. CAUTION: If you have two pattern pieces that are adjacent, be sure to cut one at least ¼″ larger than the pattern calls for so that one piece is slightly underneath the other, not butted together. This makes stitching easier; you will only have to stitch the top piece where two pieces come together. (For example, on the "Let Earth Receive Her King" Advent banner the garments of the people are adjacent. One should be cut to fit underneath the other; they should not be butted together.)

7. Place all pieces on the background to be certain there is enough room for spacing.

8. Remove all pieces except for the first layer. Iron on the pieces, layer by layer, following the directions that come with Stitch Witchery. Iron on the entire banner before you begin stitching, as this produces a more even effect than stitching layer by layer.

9. Stitch the banner. For a finished look and durability, use a zigzag stitch to outline the various portions of the banner. A straight stitch may be used, but it will produce a more informal look. Adjust the zigzag stitch according to the finish desired. A closer stitch will produce a more definite outline; a more open stitch will hold the pieces in place but will not give the definite outline effect.

10. You are ready to line your banner!

LINING

When you have completed stitching the banner, determine the exact finished length you desire it to be. The sides and bottom will be stitched with a ⅝″ seam. If the top is to have a rod inserted through it, add 3 ½″ to the finished length of the banner, trimming away any excess at the top and bottom. It is important that all edges be very straight for the banner to hang evenly.

Next lay out the lining fabric on a cutting board or flat surface. Place the banner on top of the lining with the *wrong* side up. Cut the lining to the exact size of the banner and pin the two together at the sides, top, and bottom. Stitch *only* the sides and bottom together with a ⅝″ seam, leaving the top open as on a pillow case.

Trim the seams, clip the corners, and turn the banner right side out. Press it, using a damp cloth. Open it out at a side seam, right side up. Turn the seam toward the lining, and stitch as close to the seam as possible, being careful not to catch the front of the banner in the seam. Repeat for the bottom and the other side. (You will not be able to stitch all the way to the bottom because of the corner.) This is known as the Bishop Method; it holds the lining in place and prevents the edge of the lining from rolling to the front.

Turn the top raw edge of the banner and lining under ½″, stitch, and press firmly. Then turn the top under to create a 3 ½″ hem. Pin and press firmly in place. Stitch the hem in place 3″ from the top of the banner. This will form a three-inch casing for insertion of a rod.

If tabs are to be used in place of a casing for hanging the banner, these should be pinned on from the back side of the banner. Edge stitch the tabs in place, then stitch again ¼″ from the first stitching. Be certain that the tabs all measure the same length from the top of the banner so that the banner will hang evenly.

BORDERS, TABS, AND LITTLE EXTRAS

The addition of decorative tabs, borders, and other types of trim to the finished banner can enhance its beauty and add to the impact of its message. These finishing touches have been drawn into most of the designs or have been suggested along with the banner. Use the suggested items or create your own finishing touches from these three categories:

1. **Borders.** The bottom of the banner can be much more than a straight line. Points, arches, or other indentations or alterations can add dimension to the banner or focus attention on certain of its elements. Tassels, fringe, macrame, or brightly colored ribbons can be also attached to the bottom.

2. **Tabs.** Banners can be hung by inserting a rod through a casing at the top of the banner or through tabs sewn across the top. If tabs are chosen, the color should be the same as the color of the background fabric. The rod used to hang the banner should be chosen with the fabric of the banner in mind. A wooden rod is best with banners that have rough textures or simple fabric; a brass rod would be more suitable for banners with dressy or formal materials.

3. **Little Extras.** The bottom of the banner can be functional as well as decorative. Each banner includes suggestions for trim. When possible, the trim should emphasize the message of the banner. (For example, NIKA across the bottom of "There Was Never Love Like This" [Good Friday, page 25] enforces the belief that Christ was victorious over death.) Here are several possibilities, but use your imagination to come up with your own innovative ideas:

> Camel bells
> Musical instruments
> Crowns
> Nails (or railroad spikes)
> Butterflies
> Greek letters
> Fish
> Macrame symbols
> Stitched and stuffed items such as hearts or circles
> Stained or colored glass pieces
> Brass bells
> Seashells (Baptism)
> Crosses
> Doves
> Flowers
> Keys
> Triangles
> Plastic, wood, or metal geometric shapes

Prepare Him Room

A voice cries: "In the wilderness prepare the way of the Lord; make straight in the desert a highway for our God."

(Is. 40:3)

dark turquoise star

white

royal purple background

SUGGESTED FABRICS: Medium weight fabric such as chino for star, hillsides, and path; heavy white fabric such as chino or heavy satin for CHI RHO. Medium to heavy weight purple for background. Medium to heavy weight fabric for letters.

magenta letters

bright yellow

bright green

PREPARE YE THE WAY

As the voice of the prophet Isaiah echoes across the centuries, "Prepare the way of the Lord," we hear the call to prepare our hearts for the coming of Christ. Although the road that lies before each of us may hold entanglements and obstacles that block our efforts and divert our energies at every turn, we still hear the gentle call to prepare a way for Him. This season of the year has its share of entanglements and obstacles to divert our minds from Him, but as we fix our gaze on the straight path toward the great light shining on the horizon, bearing the Greek letters for His name, *chi* (X) and *rho* (P), we are reminded of the One who has already prepared the way for us, the Light of the world, the Christ.

It would be appropriate to use the song from the musical *Godspell*, "Prepare Ye the Way of the Lord," as a processional call to worship or as part of the services during the Sundays of Advent in conjunction with this banner.

ADVENT

Lift up your heads, O gates!
And be lifted up, O ancient doors!
That the King of glory may come in.

(Ps. 24:7)

green

yellow

royal purple

magenta

tan

green

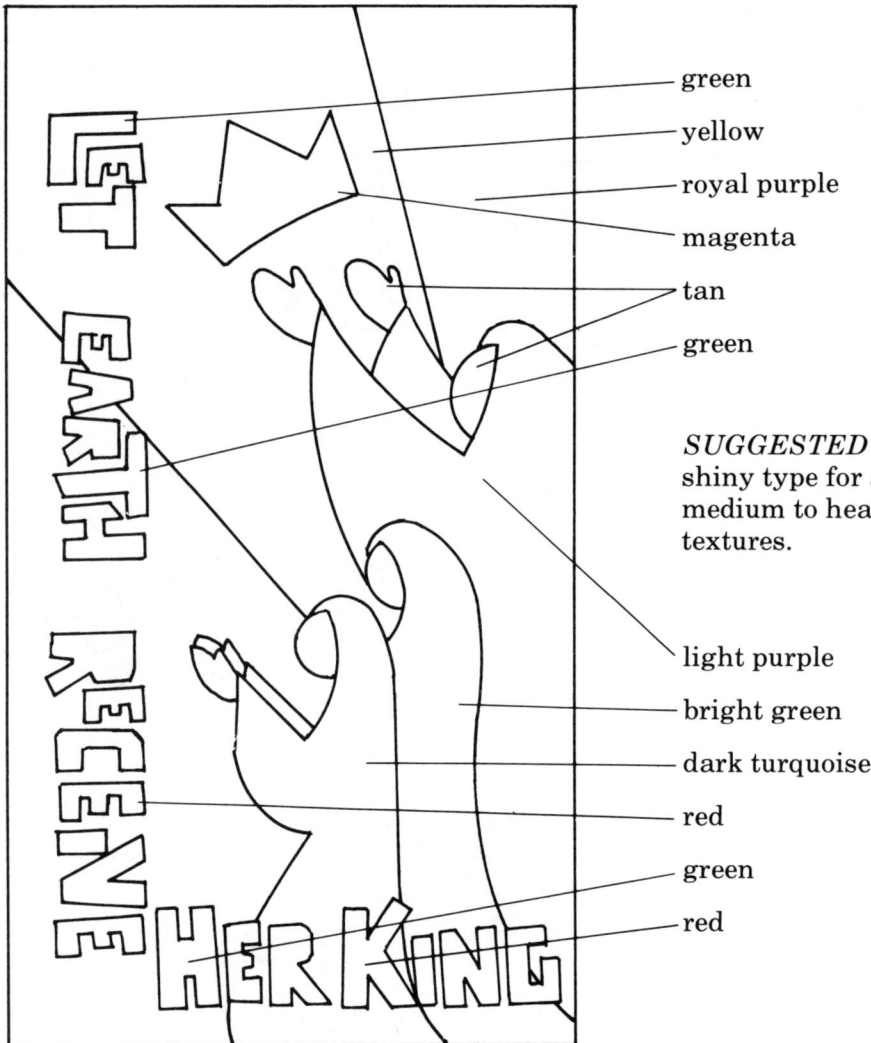

SUGGESTED FABRICS: Taffeta or other shiny type for shaft of light; all other fabrics medium to heavy weight with variety of textures.

light purple

bright green

dark turquoise

red

green

red

The yellow shaft of light beams continuously from heaven, symbolizing Christ's readiness to enter our lives. The worshipers, representing God's people, open their hearts and reach toward the Lifegiver, signifying their willingness to receive Him as King. The crown represents the kingly role of Christ and His right to lordship of our lives.

"Let Earth Receive Her King," a portion of the favorite Christmas carol, "Joy to the World," inspires the message of this banner.

For unto us a Child is born, unto us a Son is given, and the government shall be upon His shoulder, and His name shall be called "Wonderful, Counselor, The mighty God, The everlasting Father, The Prince of Peace."

(Is. 9:6 KJV)

dark turquoise

light violet background

gold

red

SUGGESTED FABRICS: Medium weight, shiny fabrics in vivid colors (such as satin, chino, quiana) for letters; medium weight chino, broadcloth, etc., for background and starburst. Use shimmery tassels for bottom trim.

royal purple starburst

green

fuchsia

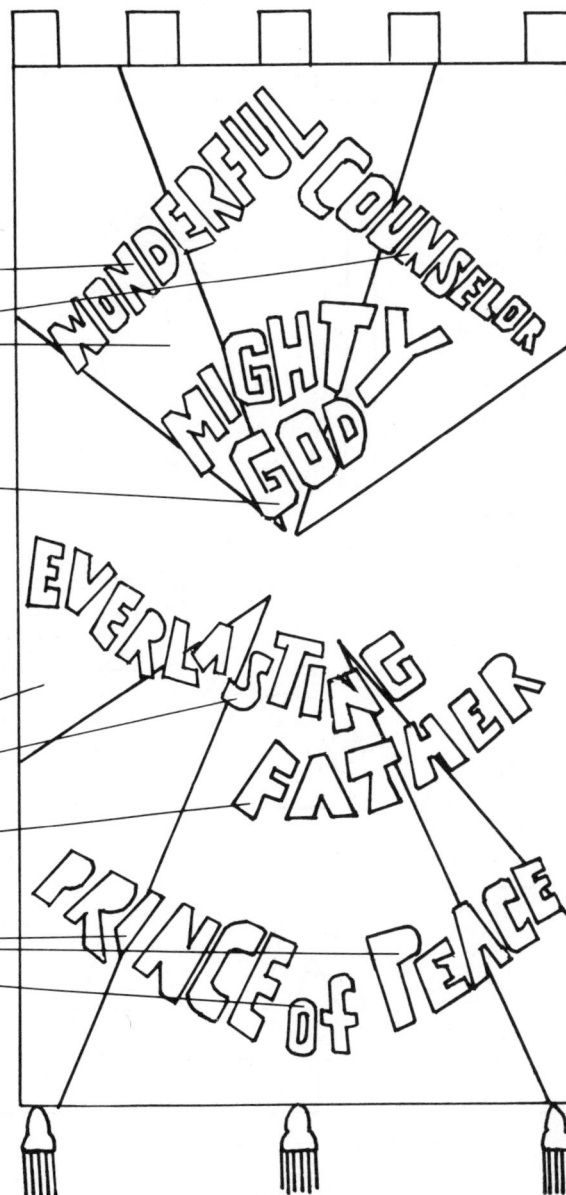

The prophets of old repeatedly foretold the coming of the promised hope of Israel, the long-awaited Messiah. Speaking through Isaiah the prophet, God promised to save His people through the birth of a Child who would personify the character of God Himself, becoming to the people a Wonderful Counselor, a Mighty God, an Everlasting Father, a Prince of Peace.

The background in this banner symbolizes the jubilant sound of the trumpet of the ages heralding the birth of hope for mankind. One can almost hear the joyful strains of Handel's *Messiah* reverberating the many names which describe the King, the Child who was to come.

And the Word became flesh and dwelt among us, full of grace and truth; we have beheld His glory, glory as of the only Son from the Father (John 1:14).

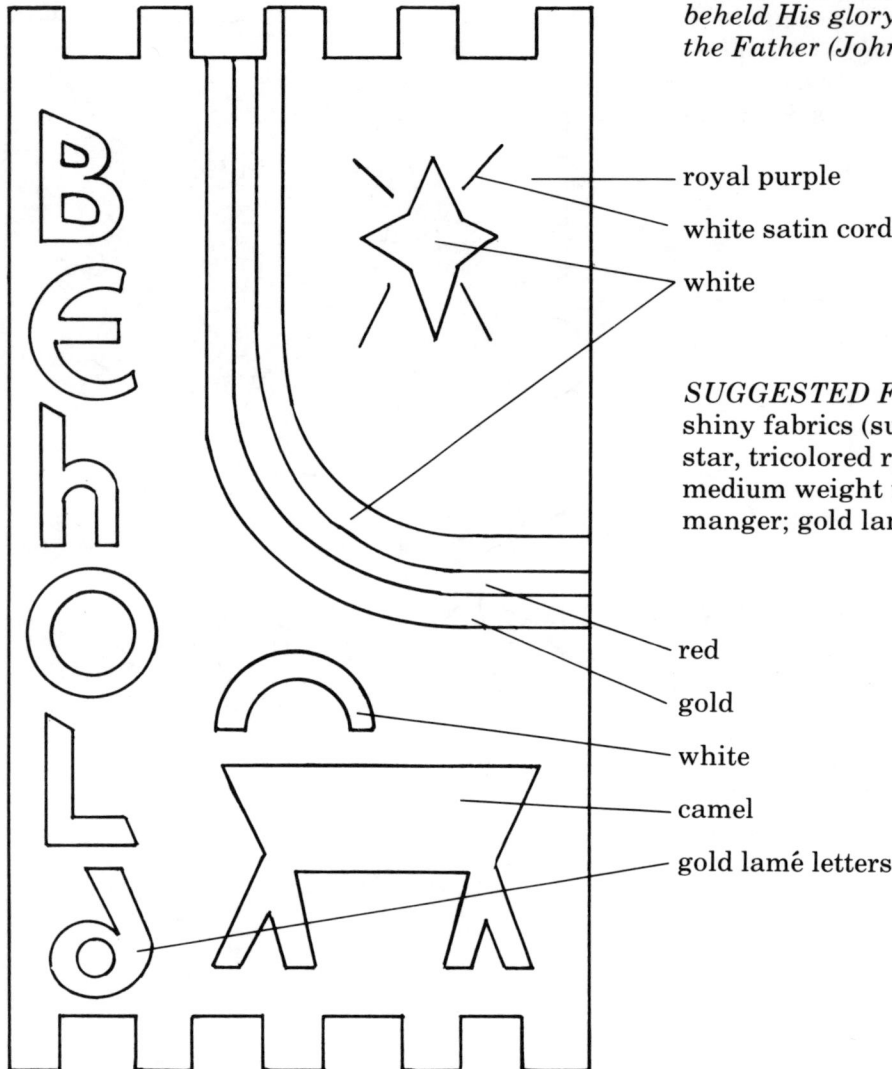

royal purple

white satin cord

white

SUGGESTED FABRICS: Medium weight shiny fabrics (such as satin, chino, etc.) for star, tricolored ray, and nimbus; coarse medium weight upholstery-type fabric for manger; gold lamé for letters.

red

gold

white

camel

gold lamé letters

The Christmas story tells us that God acted. To a darkened world, symbolized by the dark royal purple background, He sent a Light that the darkness could not overcome. In this banner we see symbolically the result of His love and His desire for harmony with His creation.

The tricolored ray emanating earthward from heaven represents three aspects of Christ's nature: gold for His divinity, red for His humanity, and white for His righteousness.

The four-pointed star and the manger with nimbus illustrate the reality of His action, the birth of His Son, Jesus Christ.

The simple word "Behold" expresses our response of awe to God's gift of love.

Glory to God in the highest, and on earth peace among men with whom He is pleased!
(Luke 2:14)

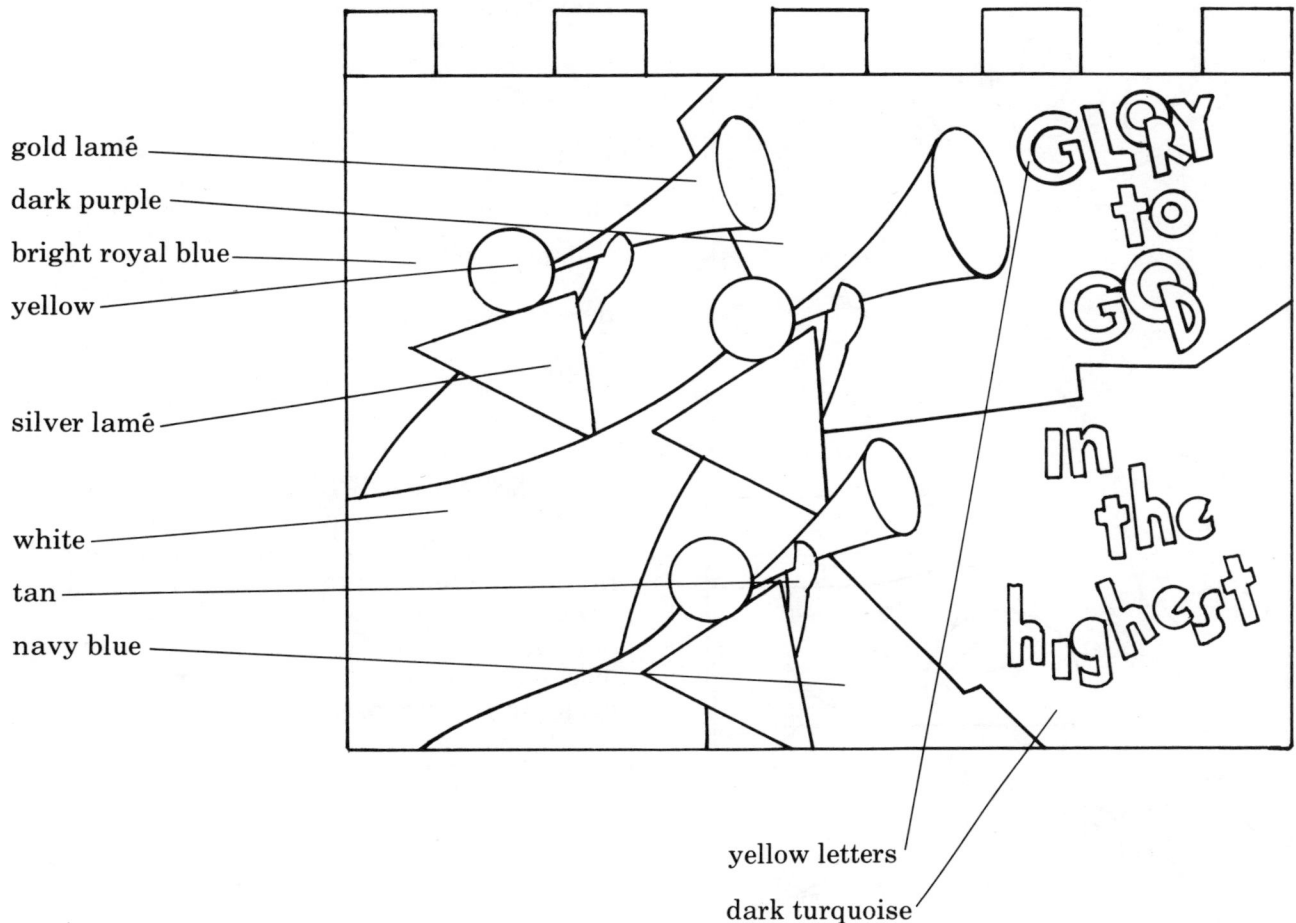

gold lamé

dark purple

bright royal blue

yellow

silver lamé

white

tan

navy blue

GLORY to GOD in the highest

yellow letters

dark turquoise

SUGGESTED FABRICS: Background fabrics should be medium to heavy weight broadcloth, chino, or upholstery. The angels' gowns are white chino or other shiny fabric; their heads are shiny yellow chino or taffeta; their hands are tan medium weight fabric; the trumpets are gold lamé; the angels' wings are silver lamé, and the letters are shiny chino, etc. Attractive trim for the bottom would be Christmas-tree-ornament trumpets.

The same gladness that seized the shepherds on the hillsides of Judea that first Christmas night is rekindled within us each Christmas. The good news of Christ's birth stirs wonder and amazement anew at the completeness of God's love.

The trumpets of the heavenly hosts shatter the stillness of the night, as indicated by the broken lines of the background sky. They proclaim the glad tidings of Christ's birth, while inspiring praise and glory to God.

Go and Tell

EPIPHANY

When the angels went away from them into heaven, the shepherds said to one another, "Let us go over to Bethlehem and see this thing that has happened, which the Lord has made known to us."

(Luke 2:15)

white

emerald green

yellow gold

dark brown

white

deep gold

SUGGESTED FABRICS: Medium weight fabric such as chino for green and white backgrounds. Taffeta or similar high sheen fabric for yellow background and the words "and Tell." Rough-textured fabric for crook and inside crown. Velveteen for crown and pieces of jewelry to decorate crown. Camel bells can be purchased at arts-and-crafts or novelty stores.

jewel trim

dark brown

yellow gold

emerald green

camel bells

The season of Epiphany is the time when we move from the birth of Christ to the proclamation of the Good News of great joy to all people. The crown symbolizes Christ leaving the throne of heaven to become a Shepherd to the flock of mankind, represented by the shepherd's crook.

The faint tinkling sound of camel bells carries us back to the time of Christ's birth and reminds us of the travelers responding to the call to "go over to Bethlehem and see this thing that has happened."

Today we celebrate the season of Epiphany as we respond to the call to "Go and Tell."

An appropriate hymn which reinforces the Epiphany message is "Go Tell It on the Mountain."

Worship the King

When they saw the star, they rejoiced exceedingly with great joy; and going into the house they saw the Child with Mary His mother, and they fell down and worshiped Him.

(Matt. 2:10-11)

white

bright green

stitch black

flesh tone

silver lamé

gold lamé

flesh tone

SUGGESTED FABRICS: Medium weight chino for background. Lightly textured fabric such as kettle cloth or linen for faces and hands. Satin or similar high sheen fabric for star. Gold lamé for letters and bags of coins, silver lamé for gift box.

royal purple

red

royal blue

gold lamé

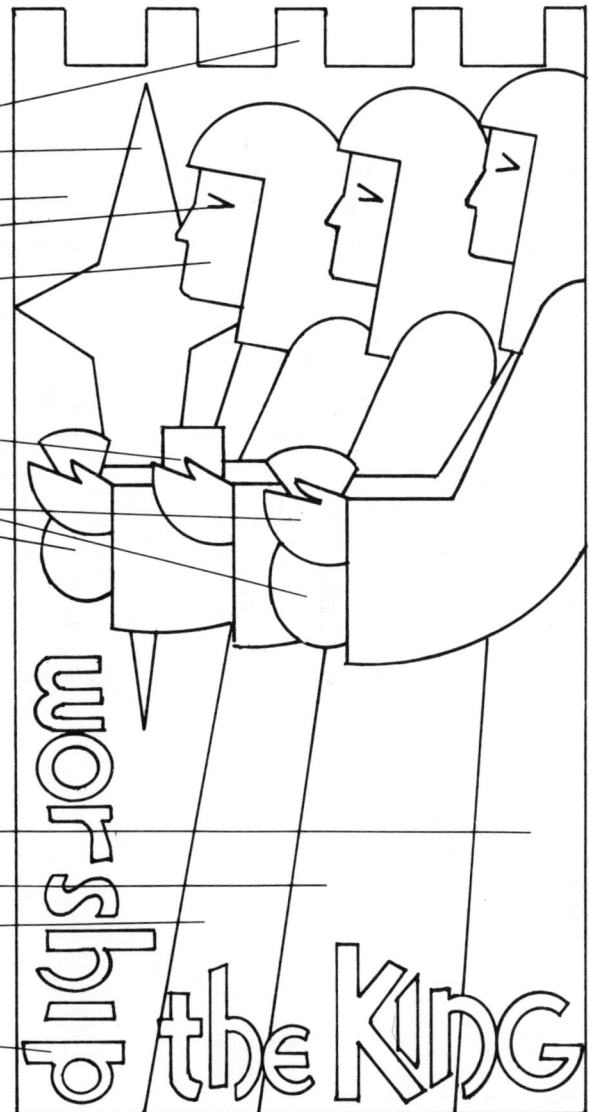

The star in the east which heralded Christ's birth shone brightly as it led the Magi to the Christ Child. In humble adoration for a King they scarcely understood, they fell down and worshiped Him with their gifts.

These first gifts freely brought to the Christ Child represent our natural response of adoration and worship to our loving King.

The message of this Epiphany banner comes from the hymn, "Oh, Worship the King."

LENT

And He withdrew from them about a stone's throw, and knelt down and prayed, "Father, if Thou art willing, remove this cup from Me; nevertheless not My will, but Thine, be done."

(Luke 22:41-42)

off-white

dark purple

blue red

dark purple

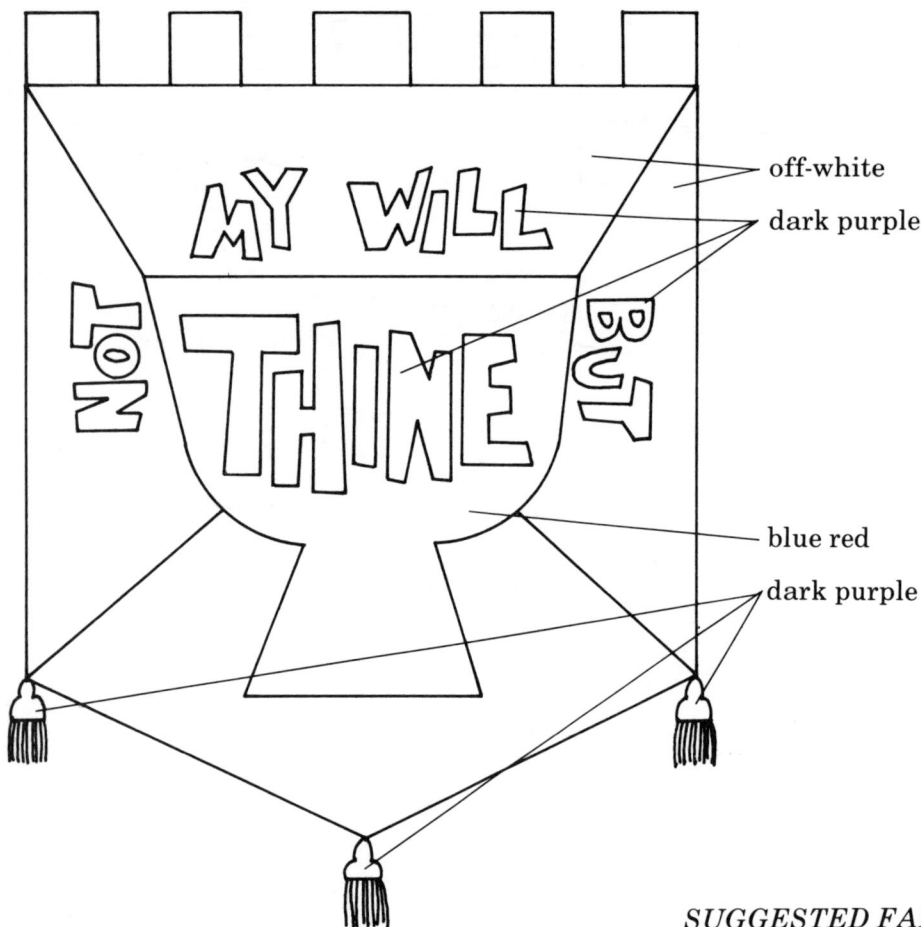

SUGGESTED FABRICS: Textured drapery-type fabric for background, broadcloth for cup, chino for letters.

In the Garden of Gethsemane our Lord experienced the agony of His mission to rescue humanity. Although He fervently prayed that His cup of suffering would be removed, He obediently yielded to the will of the Father in accepting the degrading death He had to endure. "Not My Will but Thine" is our Lenten call to complete submission to God's will in our lives.

Take Up Your Cross

And He said to all, "If any man would come after Me, let him deny himself and take up his cross daily and follow Me. For whoever would save his life will lose it; and whoever loses his life for My sake, he will save it. For what does it profit a man if he gains the whole world and loses or forfeits himself?"
(Luke 9:23-25)

light gray

brown

dark purple

light purple

white

light gray

dark purple

tan

beige

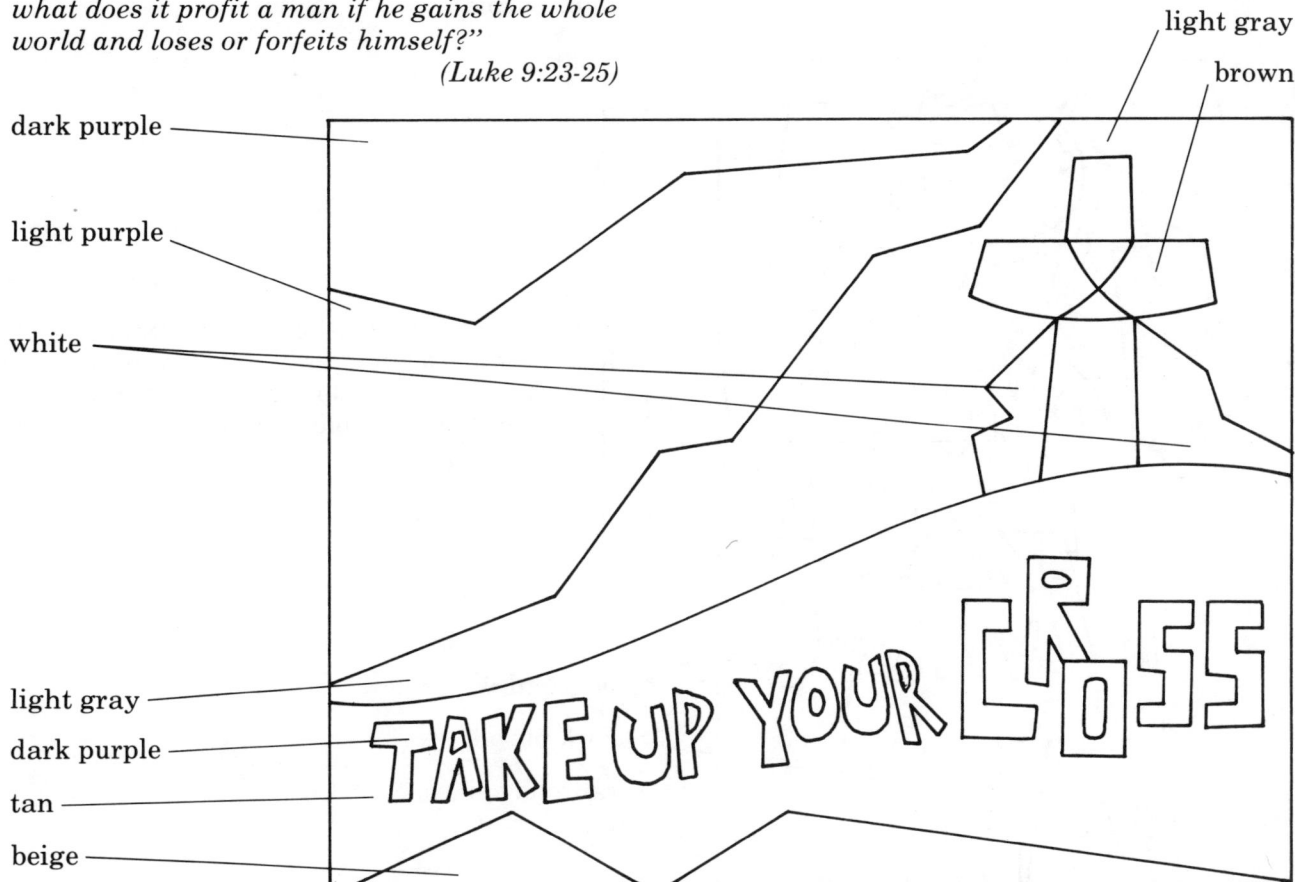

SUGGESTED FABRICS: Rough-textured fabrics for cross and hill. Medium weight fabric such as chino for sky, letters, and white light behind cross. Use cording for cross binding.

The cross stands starkly outlined against a sky of darkness and gloom, its message of death hanging heavy on our hearts. Only a small light breaks forth from behind the cross.

It is an intense light that declares to us the message of self-denial and decision. As Jesus said, if we are to be His followers, we will surely be taking up crosses daily. When they at times seem to hold disappointment or frustration, we look beyond the gloomy Good Friday cross to the victorious Easter hope. The light in our life shines as we deny self and acknowledge Christ as the authority in our lives. In this passage Jesus promises that by selflessly losing our life in service to Him, we will truly find it.

LENT

And by that will we have been sanctified through the offering of the body of Jesus Christ once for all.

(Heb. 10:10)

light purple

beige

brown

dark brown

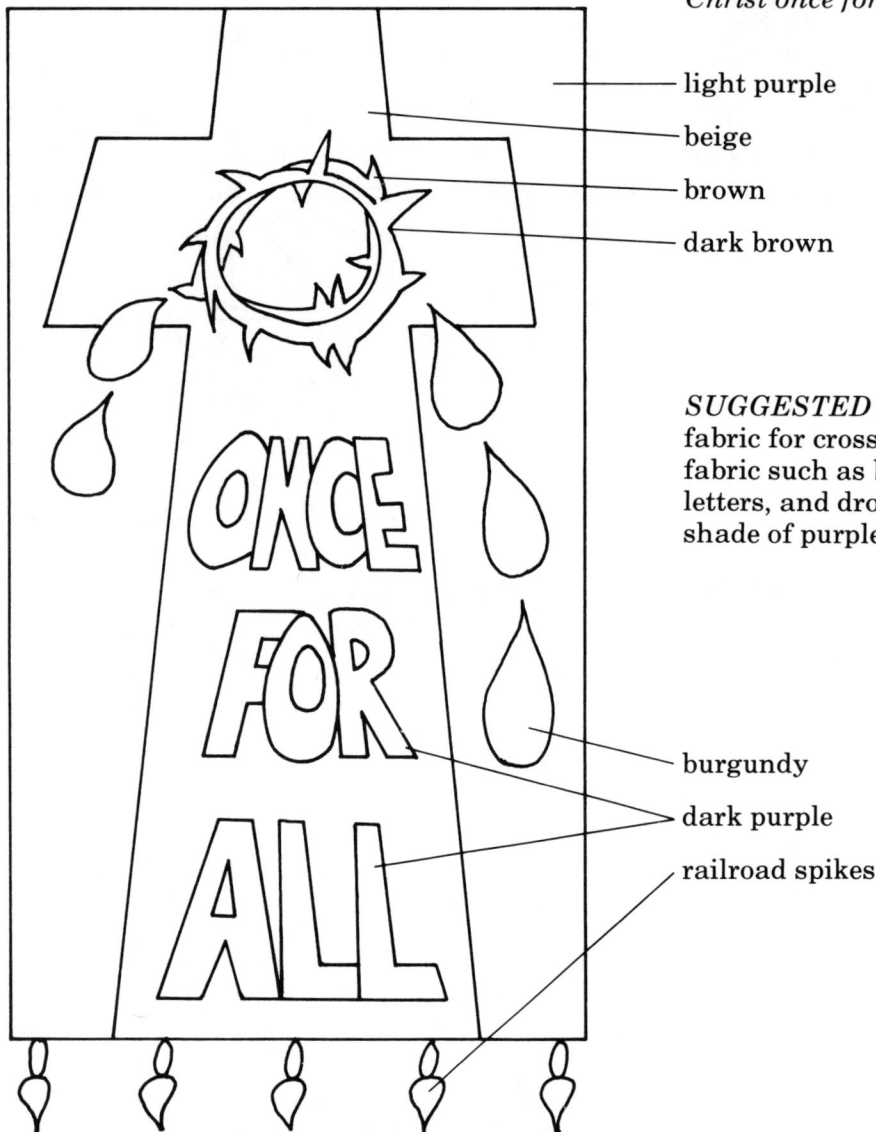

SUGGESTED FABRICS: Rough-textured fabric for cross and crown. Medium weight fabric such as broadcloth for background, letters, and drops of blood. Stitch cross in dark shade of purple.

burgundy

dark purple

railroad spikes

The cross assumes its place of prominence in this banner. The crown of thorns, drops of blood, and large nails emphasize the role of Christ as the sacrificial Lamb, a substitute for the priestly sacrifices offered in the Hebrew temple to atone for the sins of the people.

Through this offering of His sinless body, He purchased a clean slate for mankind in the eyes of God, opening forever the doors of heaven to all who believe.

The cross looms high above us, bidding us to look up and truly see what Christ has done for us.

Hosanna in the Highest! PALM SUNDAY

And the crowds that went before Him and that followed Him shouted, "Hosanna to the Son of David! Blessed is He who comes in the name of the Lord! Hosanna in the highest!"
(Matt. 21:9)

white
red orange

SUGGESTED FABRICS: Chino or dressy fabric for background, palm branch, and letters. White fringe for the bottom trim.

bright green
white

Imagine the excitement of this festive day—the road strewn with palm branches, the people waving them in the air and shouting, "Hosanna! Blessed is He who comes in the name of the Lord. Hosanna in the highest!" What a scene to have witnessed—the triumphal entry into Jerusalem of Jesus, the Son of David, in fulfillment of Messianic prophecy!

Although we were not witnesses to His triumphal entry into Jerusalem, we are witnesses to His triumphal entry into our hearts each Palm Sunday as we recall the beginning of the most dramatic week in all history.

The triumphant hosannas of Palm Sunday preface the sober events of Holy Week with joy surpassed only by the shouts of "He is risen!" on Easter morning.

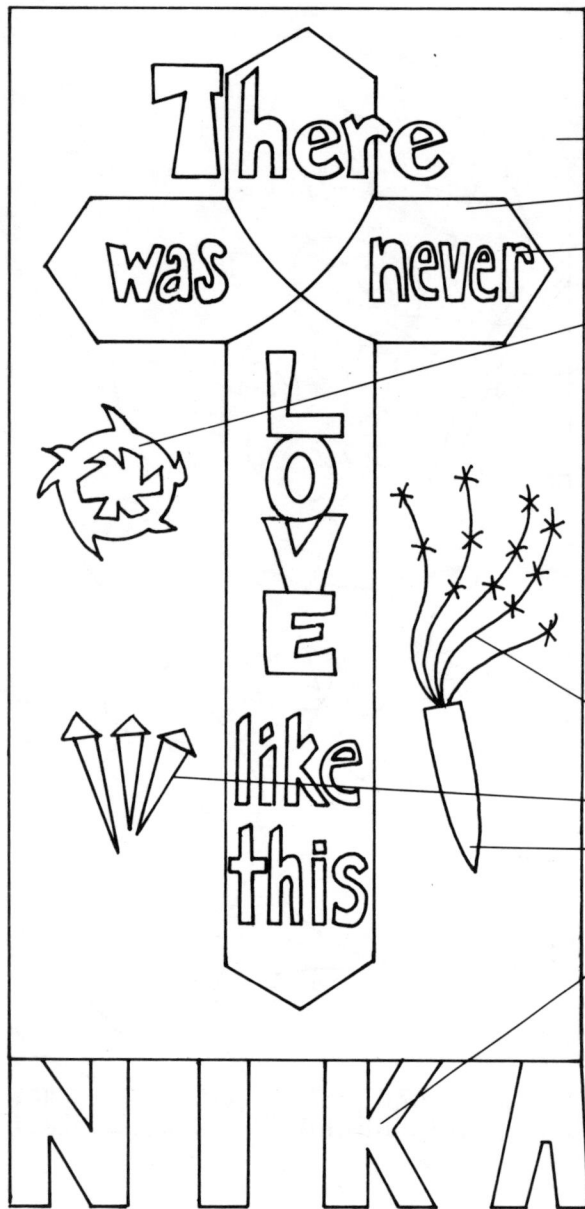

Greater love has no man than this, that a man lay down his life for his friends.

(John 15:13)

- black
- beige
- blue red
- light purple

SUGGESTED FABRICS: Rough-textured fabric for cross, crown, nails, and whip. Medium weight fabric such as broadcloth for background and letters. Cording for cross binding.

- wide beige zigzag
- grey
- tan
- off-white

(banner text: There was never LOVE like this / NIKA)

The solemn events of Good Friday are almost beyond man's comprehension. To understand the humiliation that Christ endured for us in His unmerciful flogging, the taunting as King of the Jews, and His final sacrifice as He was brutally nailed to the cross, we speak in negative terms. The words to describe this love come haltingly and clumsily to our limited minds as we struggle to understand a love we do not deserve. Quietly we stand in awe on Good Friday as we humbly acknowledge that the world has never seen such great love.

Across the bottom of this banner hangs the Greek word *NIKA*, meaning *victor*, a reminder that even in the midst of the black events of this day, hope would dawn on Easter morning.

Risen Indeed

He is not here; for He has risen, as He said. Come, see the place where He lay.

(Matt. 28:6)

orange

yellow

orange red

SUGGESTED FABRICS: Chino for the hills, medium to high sheen fabrics for the sun, sky, and letters.

kelly green

white

apple green

colored glass

Whatever reactions the events of Holy Week brought forth in the despairing disciples of that day or bring forth in doubting people of our time, the fact is boldly and forever inscribed on the heart of history—HE WON! Doubts are dispelled; gloom is erased; confidence is restored; victory is certain.

The sun appeared over the jagged peaks of the disciples' shattered dream, chasing away the pain of the past three days and in the warmth of its vibrant light restoring hope and announcing to the world that "Christ is risen indeed!" The diamond-shaped glass crystals reflect and magnify the light of this resurrection message.

EASTER

Therefore, if anyone is in Christ, he is a new creation; the old has passed away, behold, the new has come.

(2 Cor. 5:17)

white
blue
bright blue
green
orange
orange
green
yellow
red
orange

yellow
black felt
black zigzag stitch
green
red
yellow
bright blue
orange

new creation
we are the

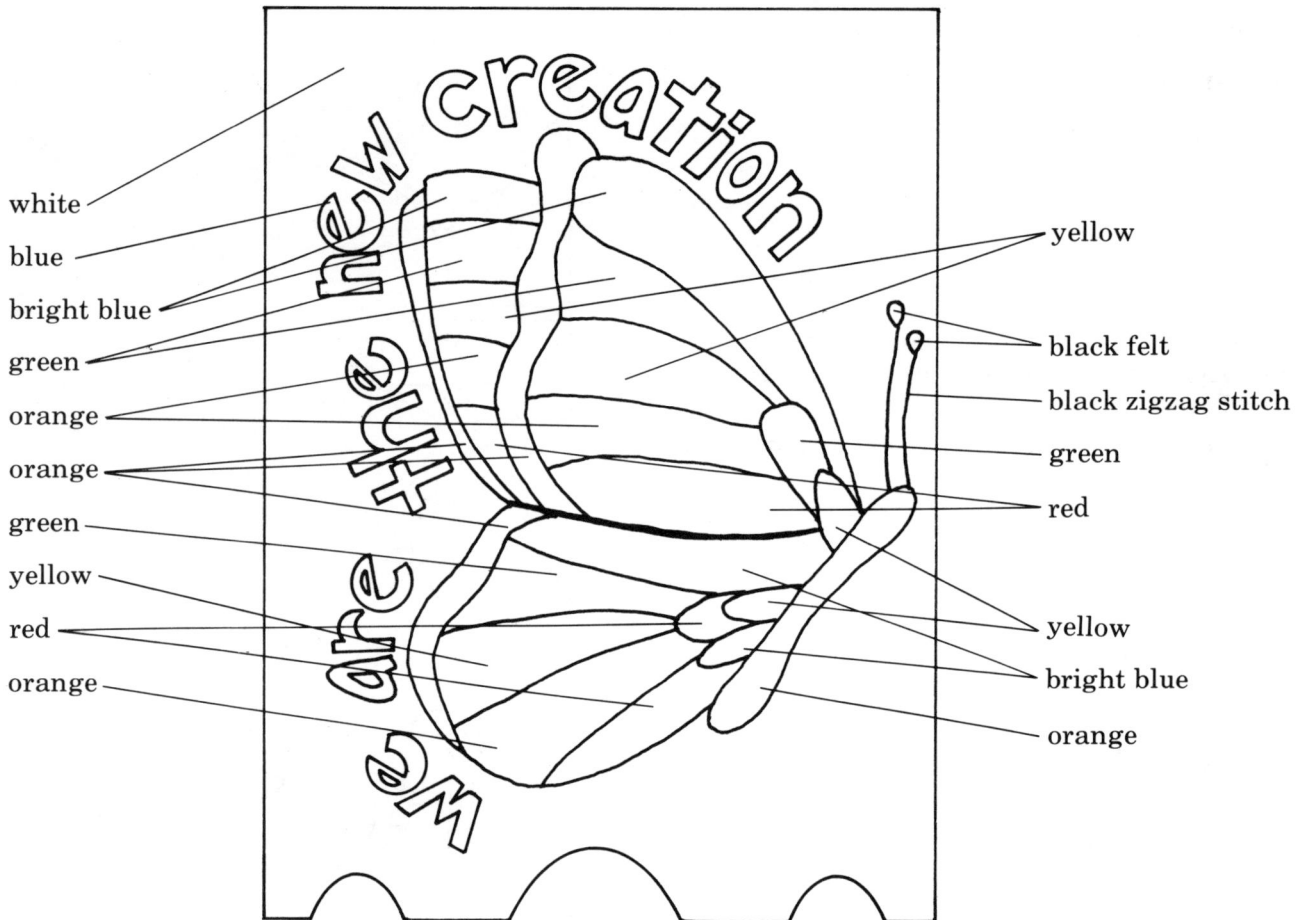

SUGGESTED FABRICS: Chino or other dressy fabric for background. Medium to high sheen fabrics for letters and butterfly. The body and wing-like appendages are one piece of orange, stitched in contrasting thread.

The lowly caterpillar reaches a stage in its limited, self-contained life when the former way is no longer adequate; it is almost as if it realizes that there is more. At that point, trusting nature to complete the cycle, it spins a cocoon in which the metamorphosis of giving up the former self to become a superior creature occurs. As assuredly as the butterfly emerges from the cocoon a more beautiful and glorious version of the original creature, Christians, too, experience their own change as they shed their old nature and emerge in the new nature of Christ.

No longer content to spend its days groveling on the ground, the butterfly now flourishes in the freedom of making its contribution to God's creation. Likewise, new creatures in Christ confidently face their circumstances on wings of victory rather than in the bonds of defeat.

Leap for Joy!

For you who fear My name the sun of righteousness shall rise, with healing in its wings. You shall go forth leaping like calves from the stall.

(Mal. 4:2)

white ———————————————————

royal blue ———————————————

bright yellow ————————————

SUGGESTED FABRICS: Medium weight fabrics such as trigger, chino, or broadcloth in vivid colors. For dressy effect, use high sheen fabrics for the symbols.

orange ————————————————

burnt orange ————————————

Like the phoenix rising out of the ashes of the somber season of Lent, the light of Easter bursts forth on the horizon of mankind's dark despair, flooding the world with hope. The outstretched arms of the suffering Christ on the cross are triumphantly transformed into the buoyant arms of a Savior lifting us into the way, the truth, and the life.

HE'S ALIVE is the energizing cry that spawned Christianity and sustains Christians today. The burnt orange ball of fire represents Christ, the "Sun of Righteousness" referred to in Scripture. The lighter orange rays, representing Christians in the world who reflect His love and light, emanate from Christ, the central source of power.

The yellow sunburst explodes with the message that HE'S ALIVE and that we can in truth "go forth leaping like calves from the stall."

MORNING HAS BROKEN

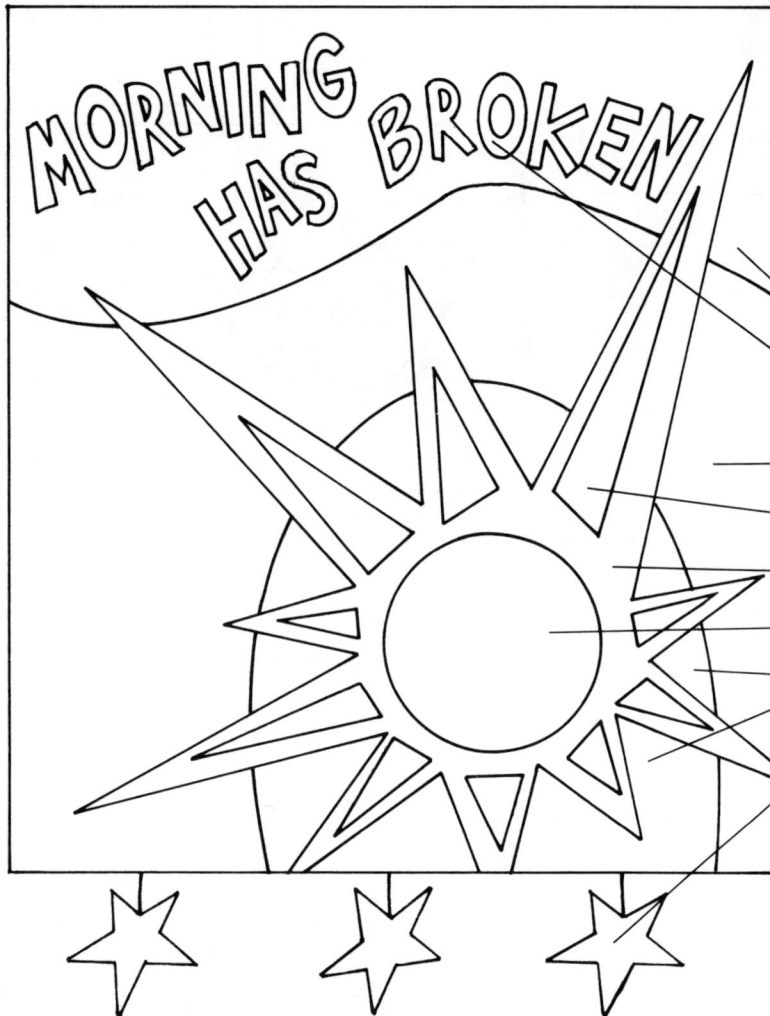

Very early on the first day of the week they went to the tomb when the sun had risen.

(Mark 16:2)

- white
- bright sky blue
- beige
- yellow
- orange
- red orange
- royal purple
- orange

SUGGESTED FABRICS: Chino for sky and letters. Rough-textured fabric for the tomb. Broadcloth for the inside of the tomb. Very high sheen fabric for the sunburst. The trim of three sunbursts should be high sheen satin (either sewn and stuffed or cut and glued to both sides of heavy cardboard).

When she arrived at the Lord's tomb, Mary was seized with despair and helplessness as she saw that it lay empty. Feel with your own heart Mary's desperation in the following moments as she unknowingly encountered Jesus:

"Woman, why are you weeping? Whom do you seek?"

"Sir, if you have carried Him away, tell me where you have laid Him, and I will take Him away."

To the woman whose life had been irrevocably changed by the truth He taught, Jesus spoke tenderly, "Mary." She turned to the One who spoke, and her heart must have quickened with joy as she recognized her Lord. Filled with wonder and amazement at Him who stood before her, she responded, "Rabboni!" (John 20:15-16).

Morning had broken for Mary Magdalene, just as it has for all who embrace the reality of life over death and light over darkness. Christ's triumph shines forth brilliantly, shattering forever the death and darkness of the tomb.

Come, Holy Spirit

I baptize you with water for repentance, but He who is coming after me is mightier than I, whose sandals I am not worthy to carry; He will baptize you with the Holy Spirit and with fire.
                    (Matt. 3:11)

red

white

orange

orange red

orange red

red

white

COME HOLY SPIRIT

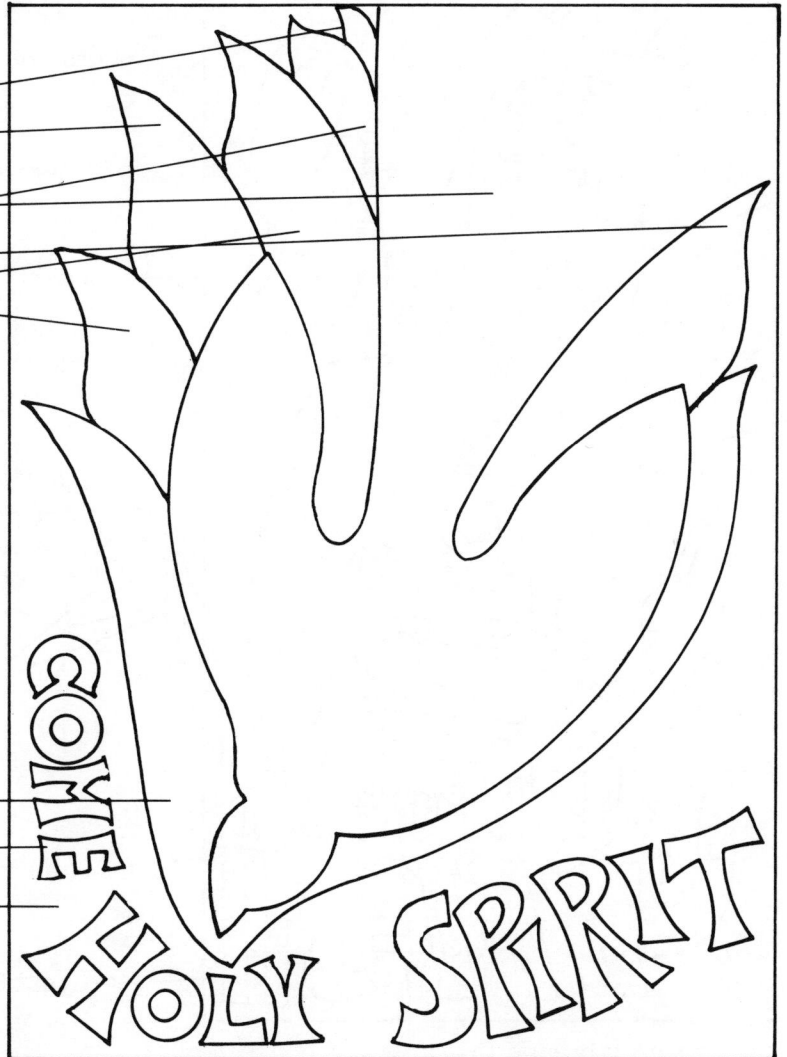

SUGGESTED FABRICS: Chino or medium sheen fabric for background, flames, and dove. Medium weight fabric such as broadcloth for letters.

Mighty winds descended from heaven, and the fires of Pentecost came to rest on the heads of the astonished disciples, signaling the birth of the Christian Church. God's generous outpouring of His Spirit, which moved these men to share the Gospel of Jesus Christ with people of such diverse backgrounds and varied languages, demonstrates His willingness to share His Spirit with all who hear His call. The Spirit penetrates and indwells the lives of Christians everywhere, manifesting Himself through the Word and sacraments for each of us as we say, "Come, Holy Spirit."

The shape of a dove, a Christian symbol for the Holy Spirit, is formed by the tongues of flame, representing the outpouring of God's Spirit on His people.

And in the last days it shall be, God declares, that I will pour out my Spirit upon all flesh.

(Acts 2:17)

— orange

— orange red

— red

SUGGESTED FABRICS: Medium weight chino or other moderate sheen fabric for flames and water. Background and letters can be any medium weight fabric.

— white

— royal blue

After Jesus' ascension the disciples banded together, continually devoted themselves to prayer, and, faithful to their promise, remained in Jerusalem until the Comforter was sent.

On the Day of Pentecost their time of waiting abruptly ended with the sudden rush of a mighty wind from heaven. As the fires of Pentecost appeared above each of them, Peter, surging with the power of the promised Holy Spirit, hastened to interpret the supernatural events to the crowd. Raising his voice, he declared that this was not a drunken revelry at nine o'clock in the morning, but the fulfillment of the prophecy spoken by Joel that God's Spirit would be poured out on all flesh, as well as the fulfillment of the promise of Jesus that the Comforter would come.

The tongues of fire fell from heaven, the Spirit was poured forth with the rush of a mighty wind, and the church was born as a living testimony to the love of God in Jesus Christ.

*The grace of the Lord Jesus Christ
and the love of God and the fellowship
of the Holy Spirit be with you all.*
(2 Cor. 13:14)

beige

white

emerald green

gold lamé

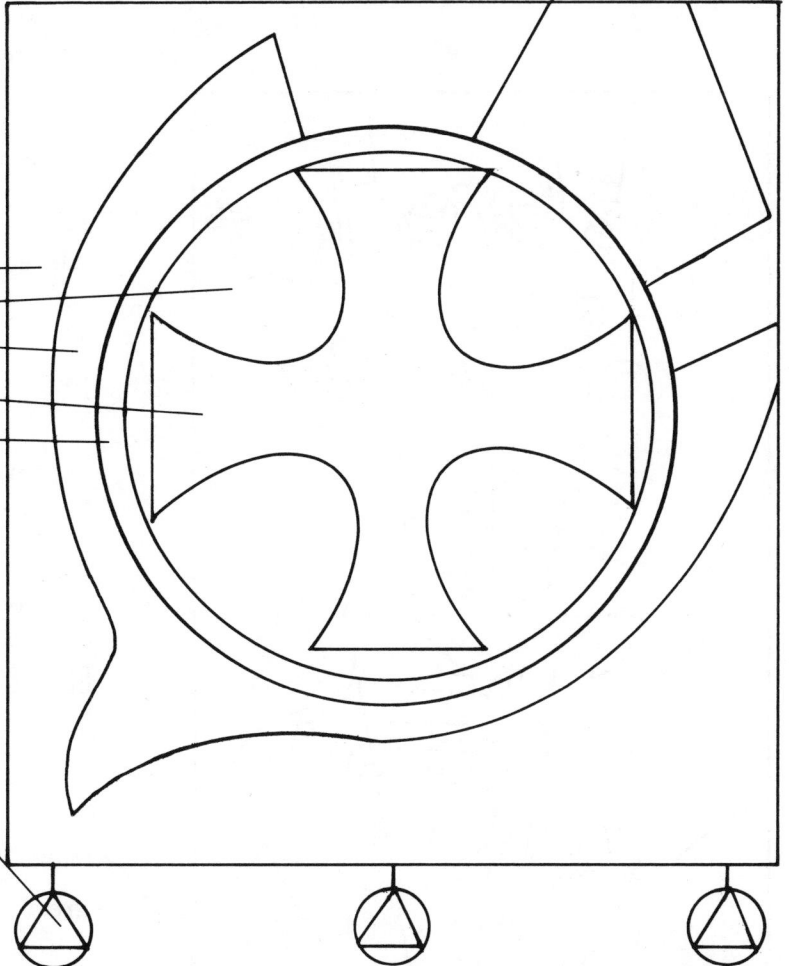

SUGGESTED FABRICS: Medium weight, high sheen fabrics such as satin, or use chino if less sheen is desired. Trinity symbols across the bottom can be done in macrame.

At the heart of the Christian faith is the belief in a triune God who deliberately reveals Himself as God the Father, God the Son, and God the Holy Spirit. The three persons of the Trinity function together with special roles in one divine purpose:

God the Father is infinite in wisdom, power, and love and is the Maker and Ruler of all things, the Almighty, the great "I Am," who was and is and ever shall be. He is represented in the banner by the circle of the Alpha and Omega, the beginning and the end.

God the Son is God manifest in the flesh,

Jesus Christ, bearing the burden of redeeming God's lost creation through His own death, thereby becoming the Savior of the world. He is represented in the banner by the symbol which has become synonymous with His name, the cross. The Father's love encompassed in the Son is shown by the circle encompassing the cross.

God the Holy Spirit, symbolized by the dove, embodies the divine presence of God in our lives, guiding, strengthening, and comforting us in time of need and perpetually reminding us of the truth of Christ.

The three triangles in circles represent the singular roles of each person of the Trinity, while the three symbols on the banner itself are superimposed, portraying the oneness of the three.

So faith, hope, love abide, these three; but the greatest of these is love.

(1 Cor. 13:13)

beige

green

white

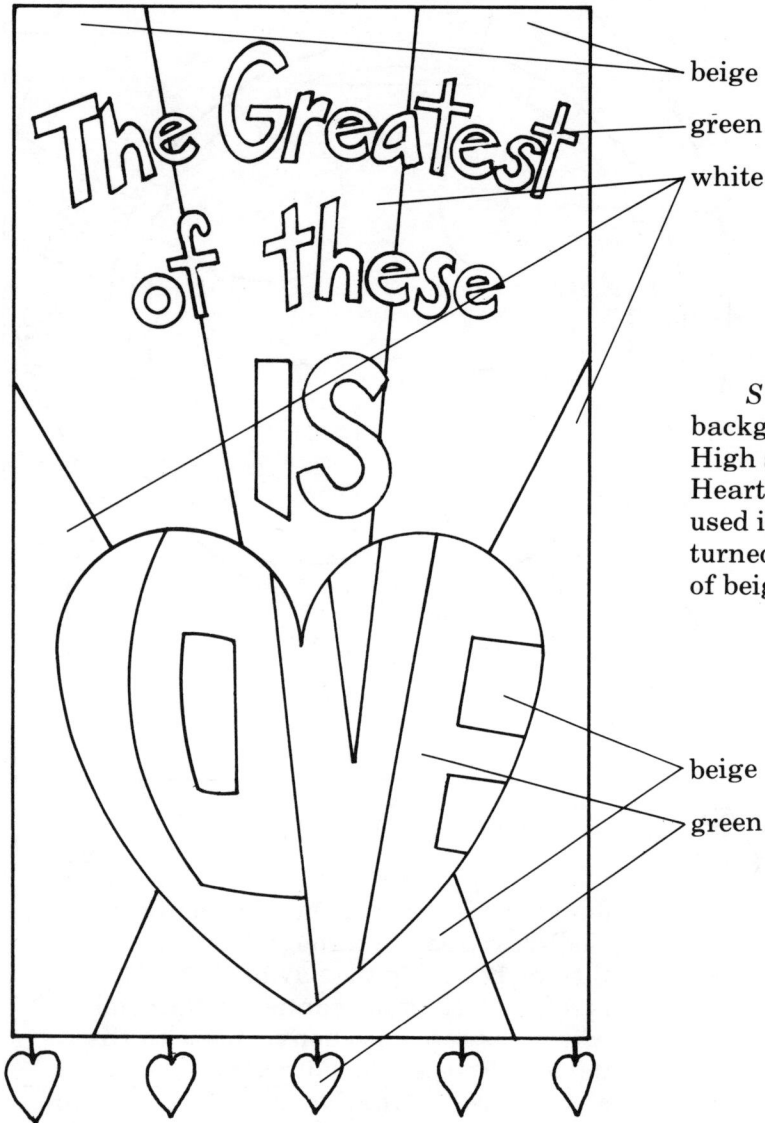

SUGGESTED FABRICS: Chino for background unless dressier fabric is desired. High sheen such as satin for letters and heart. Hearts at the bottom should be the same green used in the banner and should be sewn, turned, and lightly stuffed. Cut the heart out of beige and apply green letters to it.

beige

green

The marriage banner combines the selfless love of God, poetically described by Paul in 1 Corinthians, with the romantic love of husband and wife, represented by the heart.

God's love in the marriage is the glue that cements the relationship, allowing the romantic love to flourish, while nurturing the greater *agape* love for each other. It is this latter love that seals the marriage in a covenant protected by God.

When all other selfish love falls short, God's selfless love sustains and continuously pours life into the relationship designed for husband and wife.

Two Become One

"For this reason a man shall leave his father and mother and be joined to his wife, and the two shall become one flesh." So they are no longer two but one flesh.

(Mark 10:7-8)

ivory

green

gold lame

light camél

ivory

SUGGESTED FABRICS: Gold lamé as specified. Satin or other high sheen fabric for all other parts.

white

gold lamé

brass rings

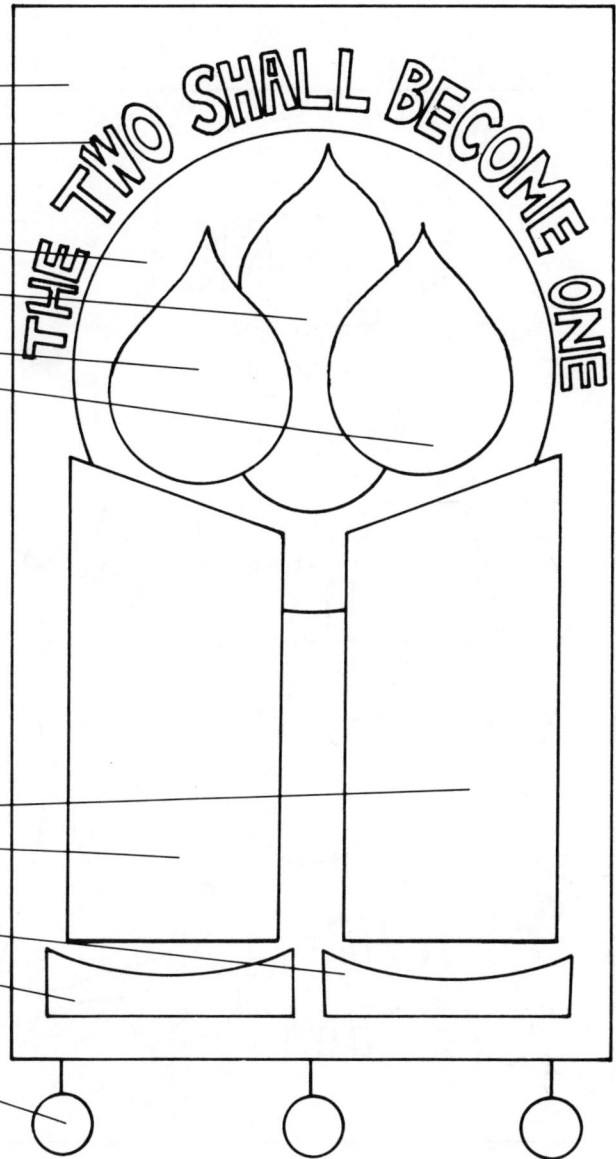

The marriage banner portrays the union of two lives, blended in matrimony, becoming one with the Creator of that holy union.

The two distinct flames, representing the separate natures of man and woman, voluntarily fuse into the greater flame, signifying that the two have become one in Christ. The circle encompassing the flames represents the eternal nature of married love as ordained by God. The small rings across the bottom of the banner represent the outward sign of the inward love, the wedding ring.

Whoever drinks of the water that I shall give him will never thirst; the water that I shall give him will become in him a spring of water welling up to eternal life.

(John 4:14)

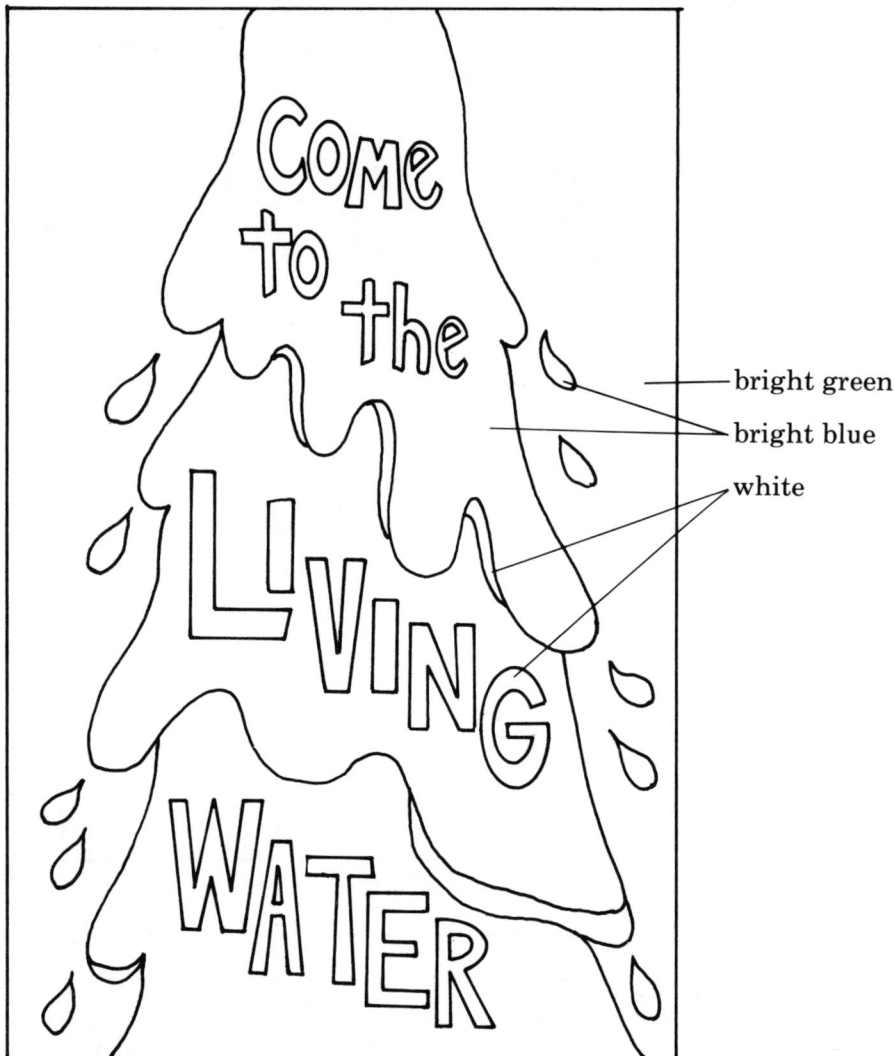

— bright green

— bright blue

— white

SUGGESTED FABRICS: Chino for all parts of the banner. Foam for the white portions of the pouring water.

Parched and withered on the desert of life, seeking an oasis to quench the thirst and ease the scorched, burning dryness of a life off course—such is man's situation when cut off from the Source of life.

"Come to the Living Water" is the invitation to the sacrament of Baptism for all who desire to drink the living water of Christ, which satisfies spiritual thirst and sustains life.

Create in Me a Clean Heart BAPTISM

*Create in me a clean heart, O God, and
put a new and right spirit within me.*

(Ps. 51:10)

bright blue

white

camel

light blue

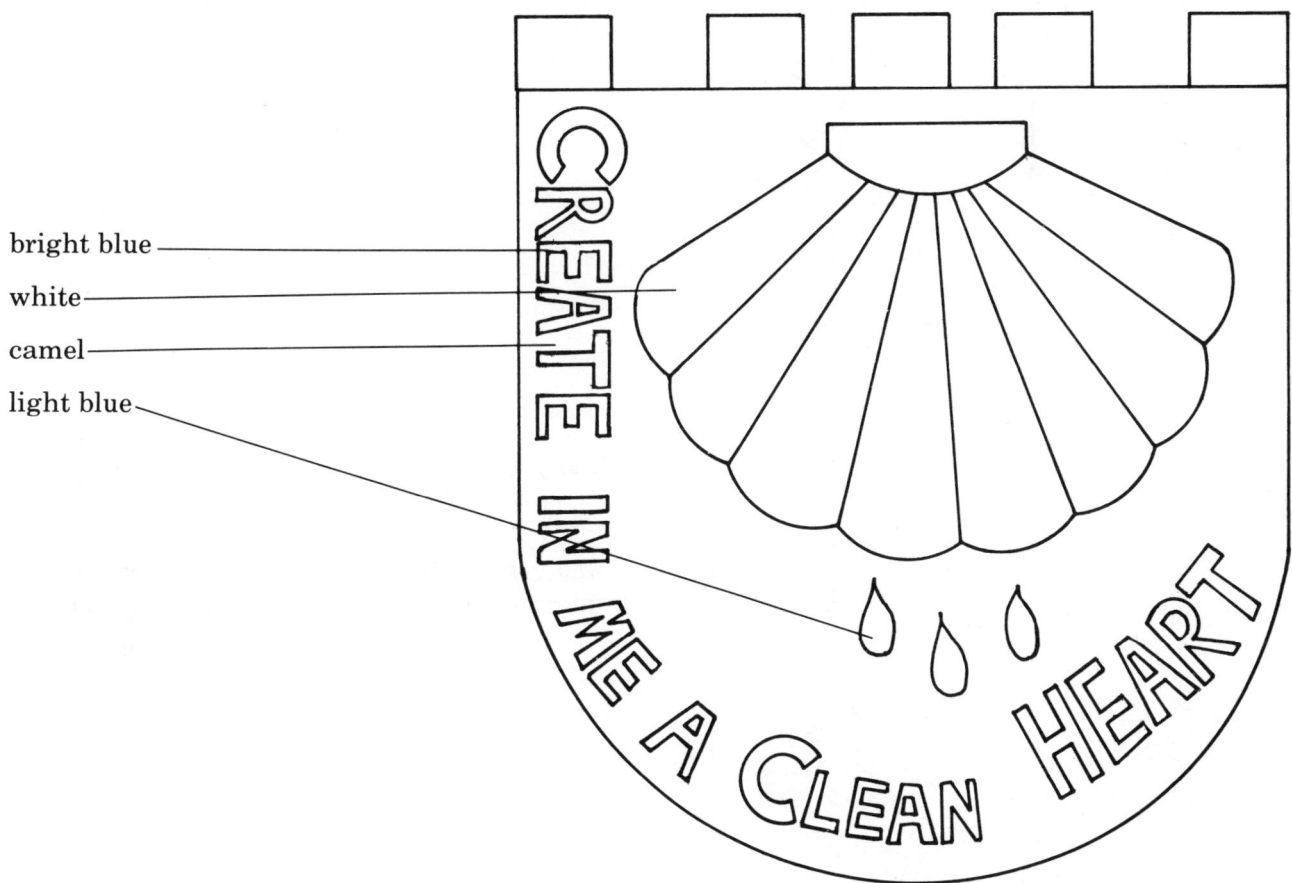

SUGGESTED FABRICS: Medium sheen
fabric such as chino for entire banner. The
shell is stark white stitched in camel.

Encumbered by his sinful nature and
falling short of a right relationship with God,
man is alienated from his Creator. From the
time of the psalmist until today, man has
sought release from his bondage and the
renewal of a right spirit within through the
cleansing of his heart. In Baptism restoration
of harmony and purification of the heart occur
through the cleansing power of God's grace.
Washed clean by water and the Spirit, we
stand before God clothed in the righteousness
of Christ.

The cleansing drops of God's grace fall
from the shell, a Christian symbol for
Baptism.

He took bread, and when He had given thanks He broke it and gave it to them, saying, "This is My body which is given for you. Do this in remembrance of Me." And likewise the cup after supper, saying, "This cup which is poured out for you is the new covenant in My blood."

(Luke 22:19-21)

- burgundy
- brown
- camel
- blue gray
- beige

SUGGESTED FABRICS: Medium weight fabric such as chino, broadcloth, or trigger.

Reclining around the table as was customary for the Passover meal, Jesus' disciples must have had strange reactions as He took the Passover bread and wine and, in complete departure from the customary ceremony, spoke the words of institution:

This is My body, broken for you—remember Me when you eat it. This is My blood, poured out for you—I am instituting today a new covenant with you—as often as you drink the wine, remember Me.

It is so natural for us, as we receive Communion, to see the cross and remember that Christ died for our sins. For the disciples, however, confused by the meaning of His mysterious actions during the Passover meal, the cross was not yet a reality. One can only imagine their amazement as the realization of what He had done became clear to them.

Acting out the drama of the Last Supper in our minds takes us back to the scene in that upper room and vividly inscribes it on our hearts, compelling us each time we "take, eat, and drink" the elements of His new covenant to "remember."

Come to the Table

COMMUNION

Now as they were eating, Jesus took bread, and blessed, and broke it, and gave it to the disciples and said, "Take, eat; this is My body." And He took a cup, and when He had given thanks He gave it to them, saying, "Drink of it, all of you; for this is My blood of the covenant, which is poured out for many for the forgiveness of sins (Matt. 26:26-28).

light violet

gold

red

white

pewter

light brown

camel

off-white

gold

brown

gold braid

self fringe

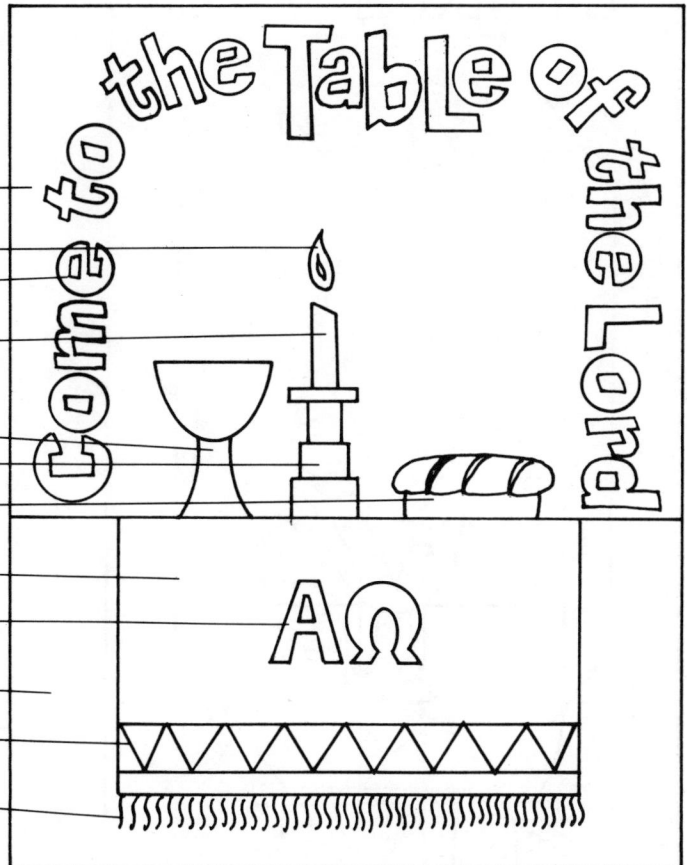

SUGGESTED FABRICS: Medium weight fabric such as broadcloth for all items except the candlestick, the table (which should resemble wood as nearly as possible), and the cloth covering the table (which should be white wool with a two-inch fringe at the bottom). The coarser fabrics are used to represent folk worship. Use a wooden rod and wooden drapery rings to hang the banner.

As the good Host welcoming His guests to the lavish feast, our Lord invites us to the incomparable feast of Holy Communion. The table awaits the presence of the Host manifested in the elements of bread and wine, Christ's very body and blood broken and poured out for us.

Completely aware of our own sin and worthlessness, we come humbly seeking and gratefully accepting His generous pardon. Forgiven, loved, and free, we depart, having shared in the Meal which continues to sustain long after the gathering is over.

CONFIRMATION

TAKE MY

LIFE

white

green

red orange

Whoever would save his life will lose it; and whoever loses his life for My sake and the Gospel's will save it.

(Mark 8:35)

SUGGESTED FABRICS: Chino or other medium sheen for the flame and the bush. Medium weight fabric such as broadcloth or trigger for the other parts.

Moses heard God's call in the commanding presence of the burning bush. God wanted him, but Moses hesitated. God had a purpose for Moses, but Moses doubted his ability to function as God's messenger and the leader of His people. God wanted Moses to surrender his life, but Moses was unwilling to trust God.

God's call to yield our lives to Him, although not always as dramatic as His call to Moses, clearly pierces the stillness of our minds. Many have heard it; some have replied. When we see ourselves as Moses saw himself—unworthy and unable—we selfishly

cling to a life that is not rightly ours, doubting that with God all things are possible. Only when we are enabled by His grace to surrender our lives to the Creator to be used for His purposes can we experience abundant living. As He releases His power in us, we leave hesitation, doubt, and unwillingness behind, no longer seeking to gain the whole world and in the process actually forfeiting our own lives.

Moses' ultimate decision to respond with "Take my life" expresses the significance of the confirmation commitment as we offer our best to the Lord.

Stand Firm

Be watchful, stand firm in your faith, be courageous, be strong (1 Cor. 16:13).

gold

green

white

SUGGESTED FABRICS: Medium weight fabrics such as chino or broadcloth. For a more dressy effect use a high sheen fabric for the anchor.

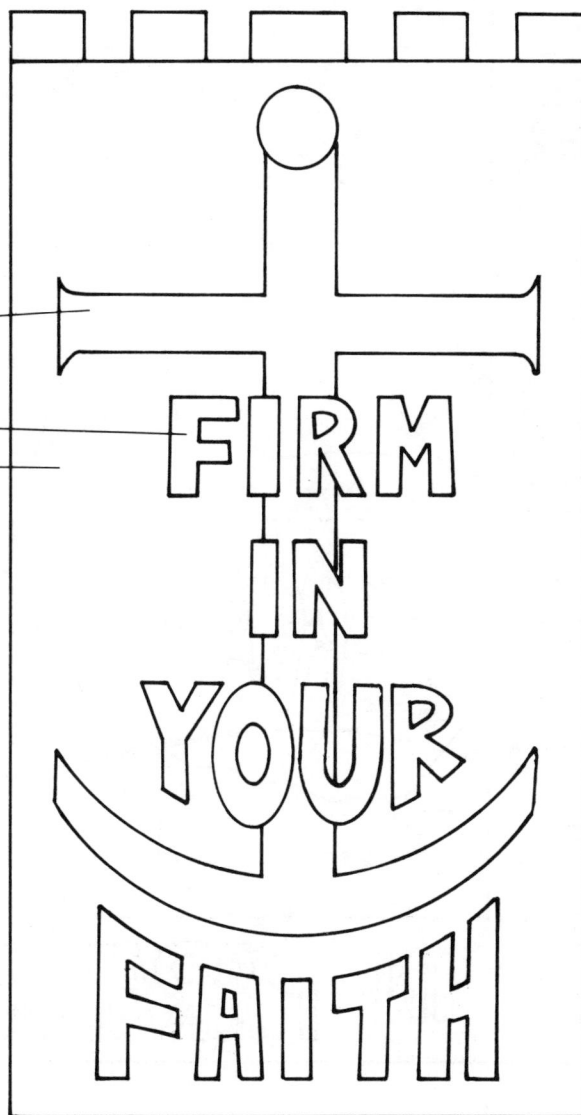

FIRM IN YOUR FAITH

A voyager floats aimlessly in an immense sea, waves of uncertainty, temptation, and loneliness lapping against his craft, each one pulling him perilously close to the edge. Lost at sea, adrift with no purposeful direction, he desperately searches for an anchor that will secure his position.

The anchor of stability we all seek is the faith we boldly affirm in the act of confirmation, a faith that securely ties us to the Father. It is not enough to let the anchor of faith down only part way into the dark waters of life. We must fully extend it, even though we often do not see its intended course, until it is firmly grounded in our sure foundation, Jesus Christ.

FUNERAL

light gray

dark peach

medium gray

charcoal gray

peach

pink

yellow

SUGGESTED FABRICS: Any medium weight, medium tone fabric for the sun and rays. Medium weight, light texture for the clouds. Medium weight such as trigger for the hills and river. Make the letters and the sun the same dark peach.

emerald green

white

apple green

bright blue

TODAY YOU WILL BE WITH ME

IN PARADISE

The death of a loved one calls forth, perhaps more than any other life-changing crisis, a myriad of conflicting emotions in those who must live with the absence of a dear and familiar face. Grasping for any and every means of solace to alleviate the burden of sorrow, a turn toward the One who conquered death itself is often the soothing balm that comforts the mourner.

Remembering Jesus' comforting words of assurance to the thief on the cross, who came to know the Savior during the last moments of his life, brings a quiet peace to the hearts of the grief-stricken mourners. His promise that "today you will be with Me in Paradise" assures all believers of an eternal place with Him.

The peace of the river in the midst of the "valley of death" and the sun shining from beneath the clouds speak for themselves in this funeral banner.

A Place Prepared

When I go and prepare a place for you, I will come again and will take you to Myself, that where I am you may be also.

(John 14:3)

peach ——————————————————

blue ——————————————————

pink ——————————————————

yellow ——————————————————

SUGGESTED FABRICS: Any medium weight fabric in pastel tones for all parts of the banner except the letters, which should be bright green. Use white narrow satin cord to hang the tassel. A quarter-inch dowel rod inserted in a casing across the bottom will allow the tassel and cord to hang properly.

bright green ——————————

green ——————————

white ——————————

I GO TO PREPARE A PLACE FOR YOU

When Jesus ascended and left His little band of followers to live in the world without Him, they must have experienced to some extent the feeling of helplessness and loss that invades the heart of a grieving person in the early hours of adjustment to life without a loved one.

Faith in His promise to go and prepare a place for us and to come and receive us into that place plants hope in the midst of despair and trust that there is life beyond death, a permanent home with the Lord and with the loved ones who have gone before.

The upward sweep of Jesus' ascension promise reminds us that in Him we move beyond death to eternal life.

What Can I Give?

Honor the Lord with your substance and with the first fruits of all your produce.

(Prov. 3:9)

— yellow

— turquoise

— black stitching or cord

— black

— white

SUGGESTED FABRICS: Medium weight fabrics such as broadcloth or trigger. Silver lamé where specified.

— white

— gold

— silver lamé

Each new morning offers us the opportunity to make our day the Lord's day by asking Him "What can I give you today, Lord?"

We wonder: Will it be my time given to someone in need or to a demanding task; my talent given in teaching a class, baking Communion bread, or witnessing to a brother; or my material possessions given to alleviate another's poverty or to support the work of those who penetrate the world with the Good News?

Turning to the Source of unconditional giving, we ask for open eyes to see the needs around us and to look for ways to respond, for ears to hear His call to tasks that further His purpose, for energy to rise to those occasions when we are asked to use our talents, and for hearts to generously support the work of His kingdom on earth with the best of the time, talents, and possessions He has so freely given.

Teach Me, Lord

Teach me, O Lord, the way of Thy statutes; and I will keep it to the end. Give me understanding, that I may keep Thy law and observe it with my whole heart.

(Ps. 119:33-34)

white

gold

fuchsia

light gray

yellow orange

ivory outlined with black stitch; flat gold cord for pages

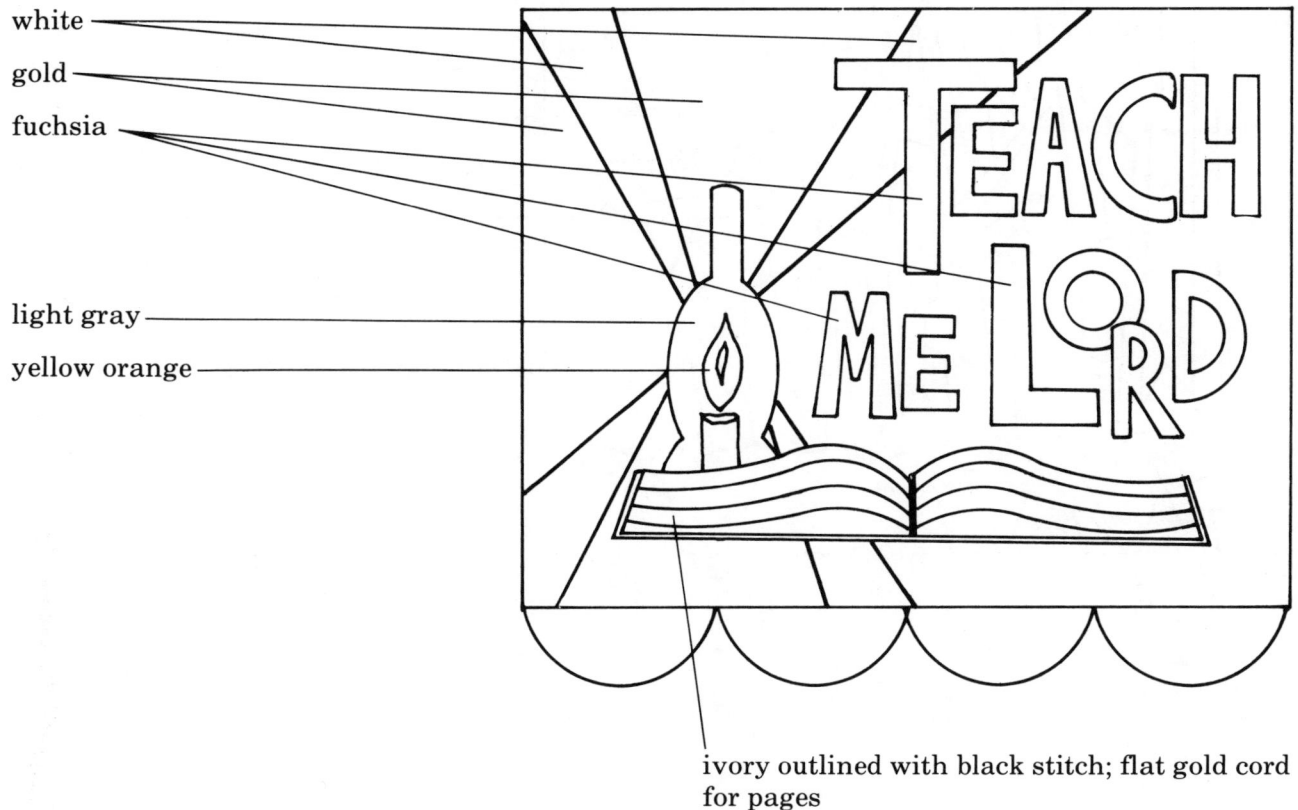

SUGGESTED FABRICS: Medium fabric for all parts of banner—chino, broadcloth, or trigger.

The open Bible beckons us to its pages filled with the knowledge of God's heart, His revelation of the key to the abundant life. To turn away from the Scriptures after accepting Christ as Lord is to cast a shadow of darkness over our spiritual growth, crippling our attempts to draw close to God. To turn to Him and implore, "Teach me, Lord," is to ask Him to unlock the hidden treasures of His word and fill the open vessel of our hearts and minds with His message.

Illuminating the entire banner is the light of truth, representing the Holy Spirit, who clarifies mysteries, imparts knowledge, and conveys truth. Guided through the Scriptures by His unerring instruction, we have access to God's wisdom and are freed from the hindrance of our limited comprehension. The lamp of knowledge liberally shines on our understanding as we come to truly know the Lord.

Praise the Lord, for the Lord is good; sing praises to His name, for He is gracious!

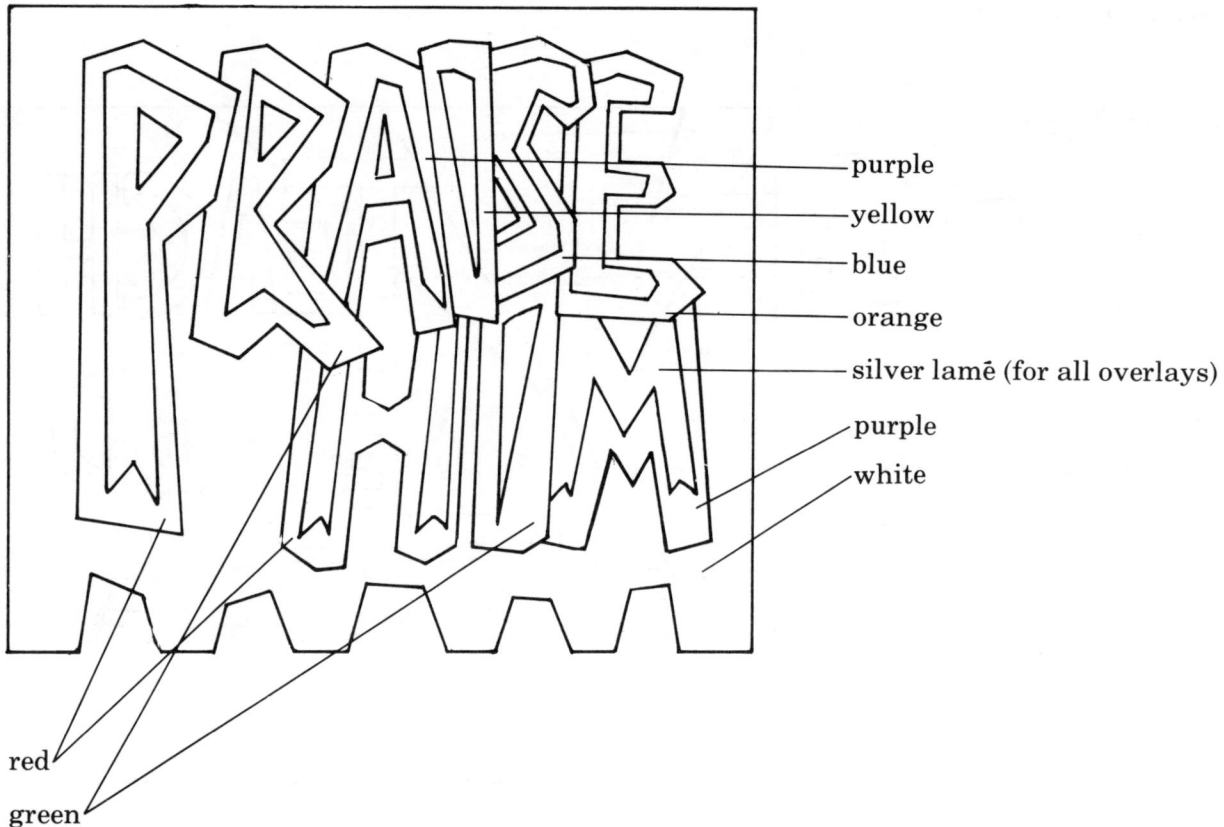

(Ps. 135:3)

- purple
- yellow
- blue
- orange
- silver lamé (for all overlays)
- purple
- white

red
green

SUGGESTED FABRICS: Satin, taffeta, or other high sheen for the letters; silver lamé for the overlays. Chino or medium weight moderate sheen for the background.

The Scriptures are laced with praise. They extol it as a vehicle of communication to exalt, applaud, acclaim, and glorify our Creator, Deliverer, Fortress, Shield, and Stronghold, to use some of the words of the psalmist.

The nature of praise is ingrained in the many expressions of worship, although praise is not confined to the formal worship service. Desiring and seeking our continual praise,

whether that be in our spontaneous daily songs of thanksgiving or in the Gloria Patri of the gathered congregation, God fills our praise with His presence.

Psalm 150 exhorts all living creatures to praise their Maker:

Praise Him with trumpet sound;
    praise Him with lute and harp!
Praise Him with timbrel and dance;
    praise Him with strings and pipe!
Praise Him with sounding cymbals;
    praise Him with loud clashing cymbals!
Let everything that breathes praise the Lord!
Praise the Lord! (vv.3-6)

We Adore Thee

O come, let us sing to the Lord; let us make a joyful noise to the Rock of our salvation!

(Ps. 95:1)

white ————————————————

light tan (outline stitch black) ——

black narrow satin cord ————

SUGGESTED FABRICS: Chino or moderate sheen for background and music staff; black felt for music notes (enlarge). Use narrow satin cord for the lines of the staff and the treble clef (glue these on), gold lamé for the trumpet, and satin or high sheen for the letters. Insert brass rods at the top and bottom.

royal blue ——

gold lamé ——

Joyful Joyful

We adore Thee

"Joyful, Joyful, We Adore Thee," the powerful hymn in which Henry Van Dyke's poem is set to the music of Beethoven's Ninth Symphony, infuses this banner with its compelling strains of magnificent gladness. Any reference to this beautiful "Ode to Joy" would be incomplete without the words of the hymn itself.

Our hearts do indeed unfold like flowers before the God of glory in the singing of this song of gladness, as we embrace the Lord of love, who dispels the clouds of sin and sadness from our lives, replacing them with immortal gladness. The wellspring of the joy of living lifts us to the joy divine, leading us sunward in the triumph song of life.

EVANGELISM

He said to him the third time, "Simon, son of John, do you love Me?" Peter was grieved because He said to him the third time, "Do you love Me?" And he said to Him, "Lord, You know everything; You know that I love You." Jesus said to him, "Feed My sheep."

(John 21:17)

green

orange

brown

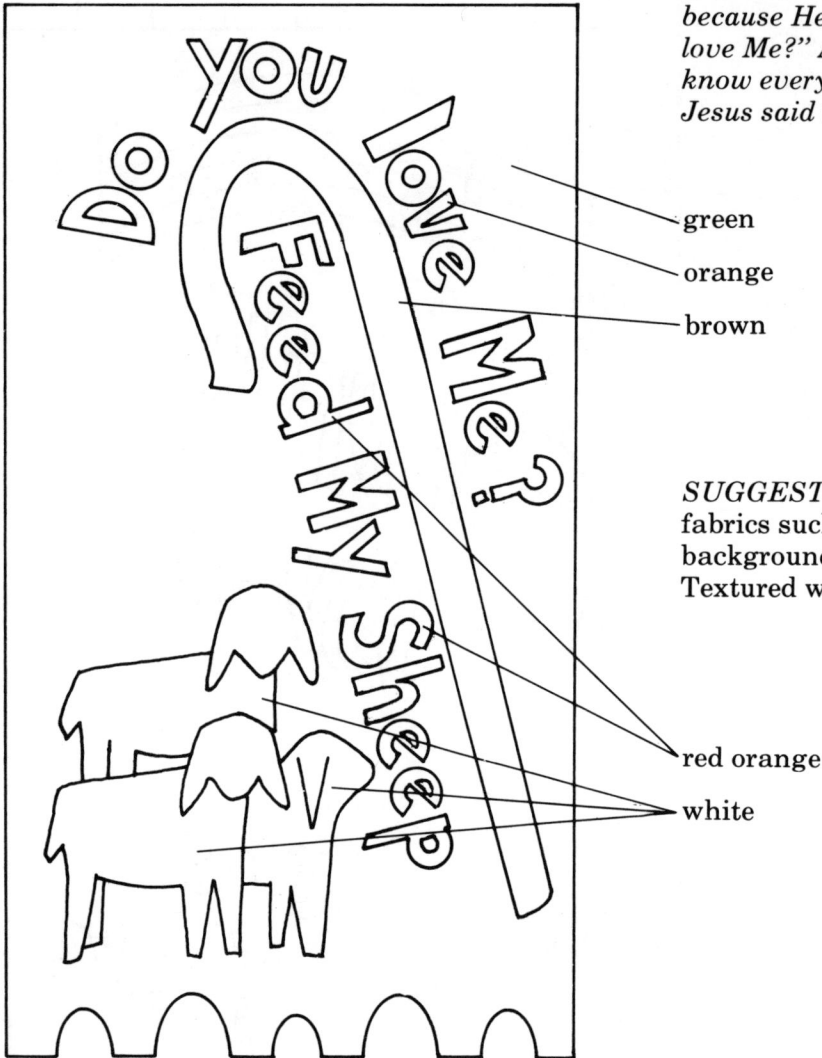

SUGGESTED FABRICS: Medium weight fabrics such as trigger or broadcloth for background, words, and shepherd's crook. Textured wool for sheep.

red orange

white

Breakfast was over. Jesus turned to Peter and asked him an unusual question: "Simon, son of John, do you love Me more than these?"

Peter was quick to respond, "Yes, Lord; You know that I love You."

A second time Jesus said to him, "Simon, son of John, do you love Me?"

Again Peter replied, "Yes, Lord; You know that I love You." And again Jesus told him to tend His sheep.

When Jesus asked him a third time, "Simon, son of John, do you love Me?" Peter, grieved that the Lord should be so uncertain of his devotion, replied, "Lord, You know everything; You know that I love You." Jesus said again, "Feed My sheep."

Yes, He was talking about men, not sheep, and He was talking not only to Peter. The pilgrimage of faith eventually leads us to the same conclusion that Peter ultimately reached: Love of God is not an end in itself; it is the inspiration that compels us to a life of feeding others with the daily bread of the Good Shepherd.

Jesus said to them, "Follow Me and I will make you become fishers of men."
(Mark 1:17)

wooden rod

rope

grommets

yellow

red

bright green

white

red, as other letters, but stitched in white

purple

bright blue

purple

large gold fishhooks

I WILL MAKE FISHERS YOU IS OF MEN

SUGGESTED FABRICS: Trigger or broadcloth—whichever produces a more vivid color.

"Follow Me," He said, "and I will make you fishers of men." Laying down their nets, without looking back, the men of the sea turned to follow in the footsteps of the Great Fisherman. Be it a walk along the shores of Galilee or into the hearts of men, they were ready, sensing somehow that they could entrust their very lives to Him.

Using the well-developed skills of their forsaken trade, now transformed by Jesus into skills they would use to cast out the nets of the Gospel, the hardy fishermen became "Fishers of Men." Across the Galilean seas to which our lives are devoted, the simple command beckons us as invitingly as it did then: "Follow Me. I will take you as you are and make you what you can be, and through you My nets will be cast into the world."

It would be appropriate to sing the hymn "Fishers of Men" in conjunction with the hanging of this banner.

By grace you have been saved through faith; and this is not your own doing, it is the gift of God.

(Eph. 2:8)

- yellow orange
- green
- yellow
- yellow orange
- black
- yellow
- white
- yellow orange
- yellow

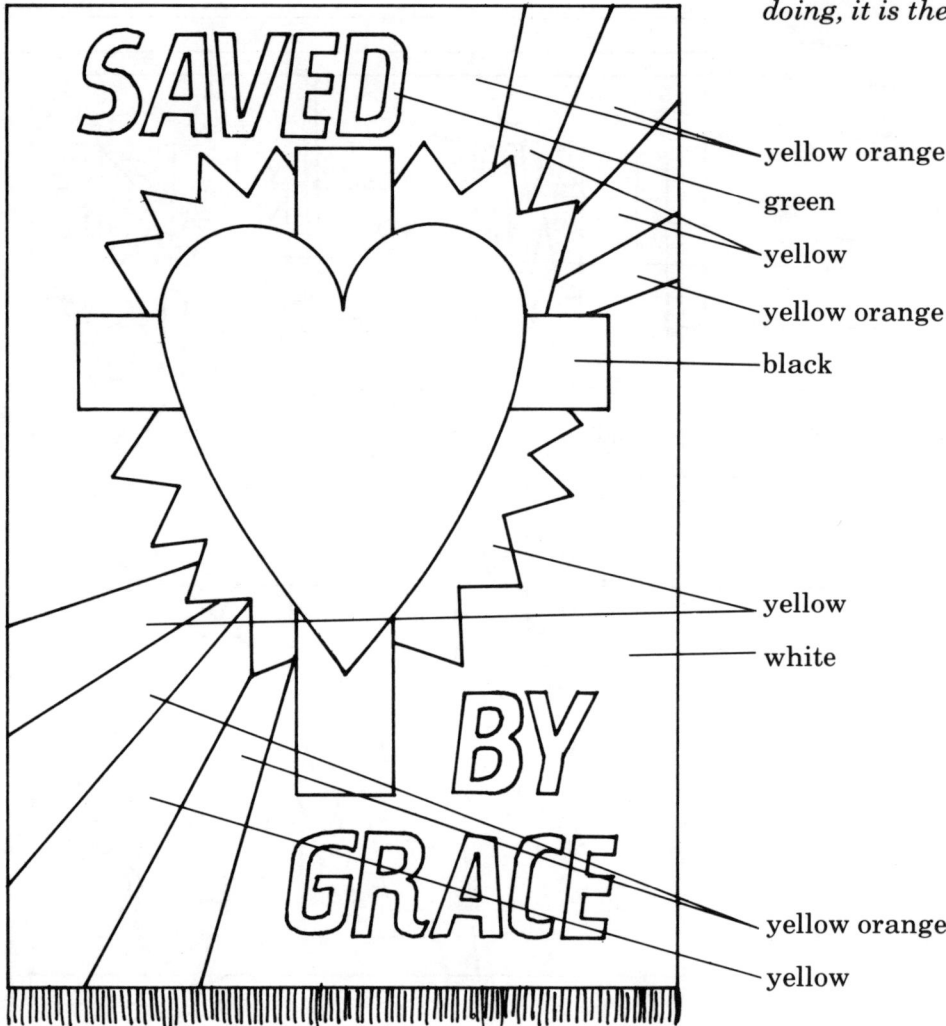

His heart singed with doubt concerning church procedures, especially the practice of purchasing indulgences to buy the soul's way into heaven, Luther zealously nailed his 95 theses to the chapel door at the University of Wittenberg. The Protestant Reformation, fueled by Paul's writings on grace, had been ignited.

Luther's beliefs and his bold fervor in the face of mighty odds continue to fire our own faith. We cannot purchase, earn, or will salvation for ourselves; to claim otherwise is to remove the power of Christ's death and resurrection. We are saved by God's freely given grace, a gift we can only receive through faith in Jesus Christ. For Luther, as well as for all believers, it is the realization of God's generous outpouring of grace in our lives that brings us to the moment of decision and carries us into action. The banner depicts God's loving gift of grace received by us through faith in our Savior. The heart, cross, and light call to mind Luther's emblem.

And I shall dwell in the house of the Lord forever.

(Ps. 23:6)

white

yellow

navy

light gray

yellow fringe

I shall dwell in the house of the Lord Forever

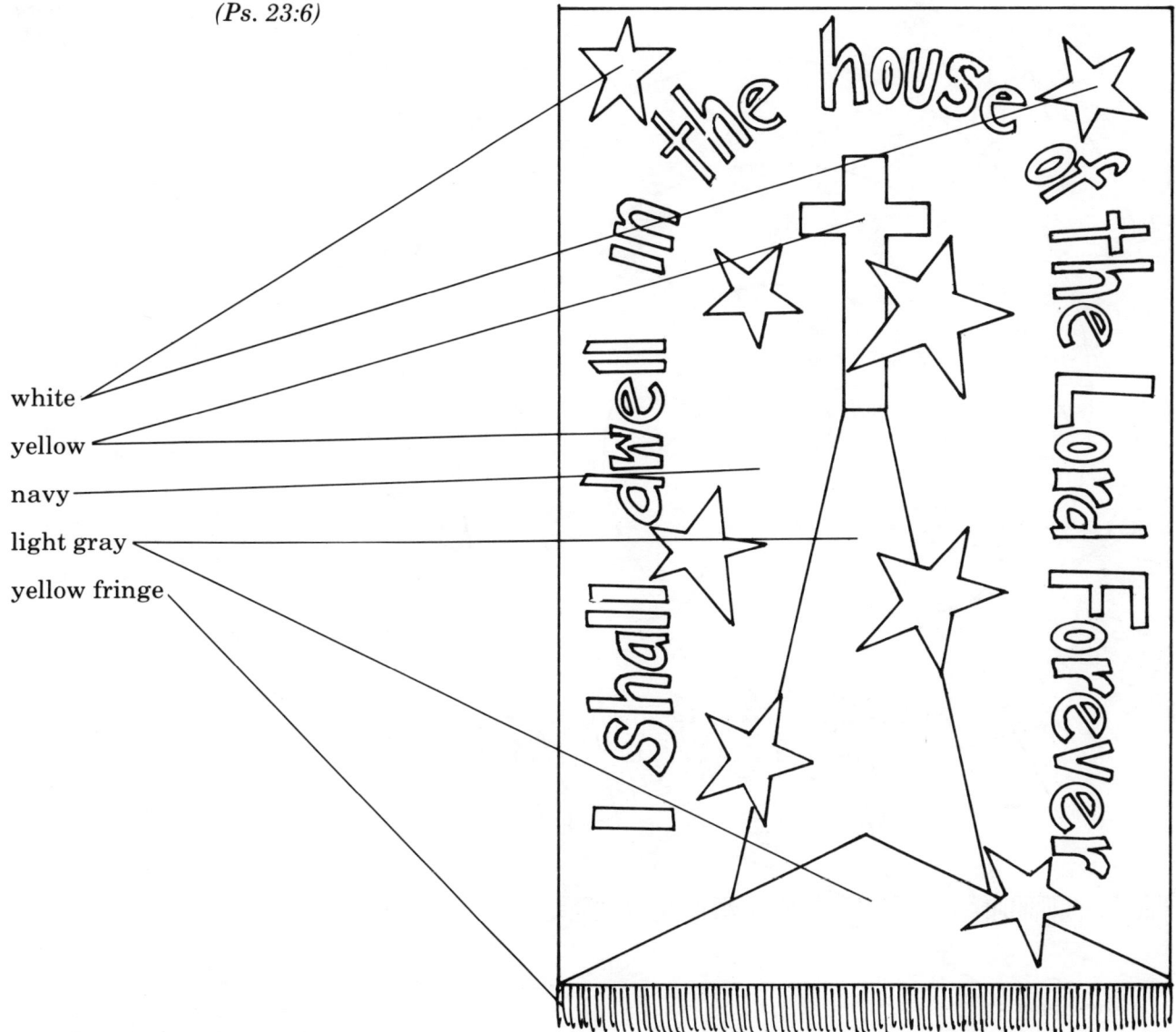

SUGGESTED FABRICS: High sheen for stars; heavy weight for cross and letters (may need to use double fabric and Stitch Witchery to prevent navy background from showing through). Medium weight fabric for background and steeple. The entire steeple should be outline-stitched in a dark contrasting color thread.

On All Saints' Day we pause to remember those godly persons who, in the living of their lives, have indelibly engraved on our hearts a lasting influence. Guided by their examples and encouraged by their faith, we offer thanksgiving to God for their lives and rest in the assurance of the joy pervading their eternal existence around His throne.

*Lo, I am with you alway,
even unto the end of the world.
Amen.
(Matt. 28:20 KJV)*

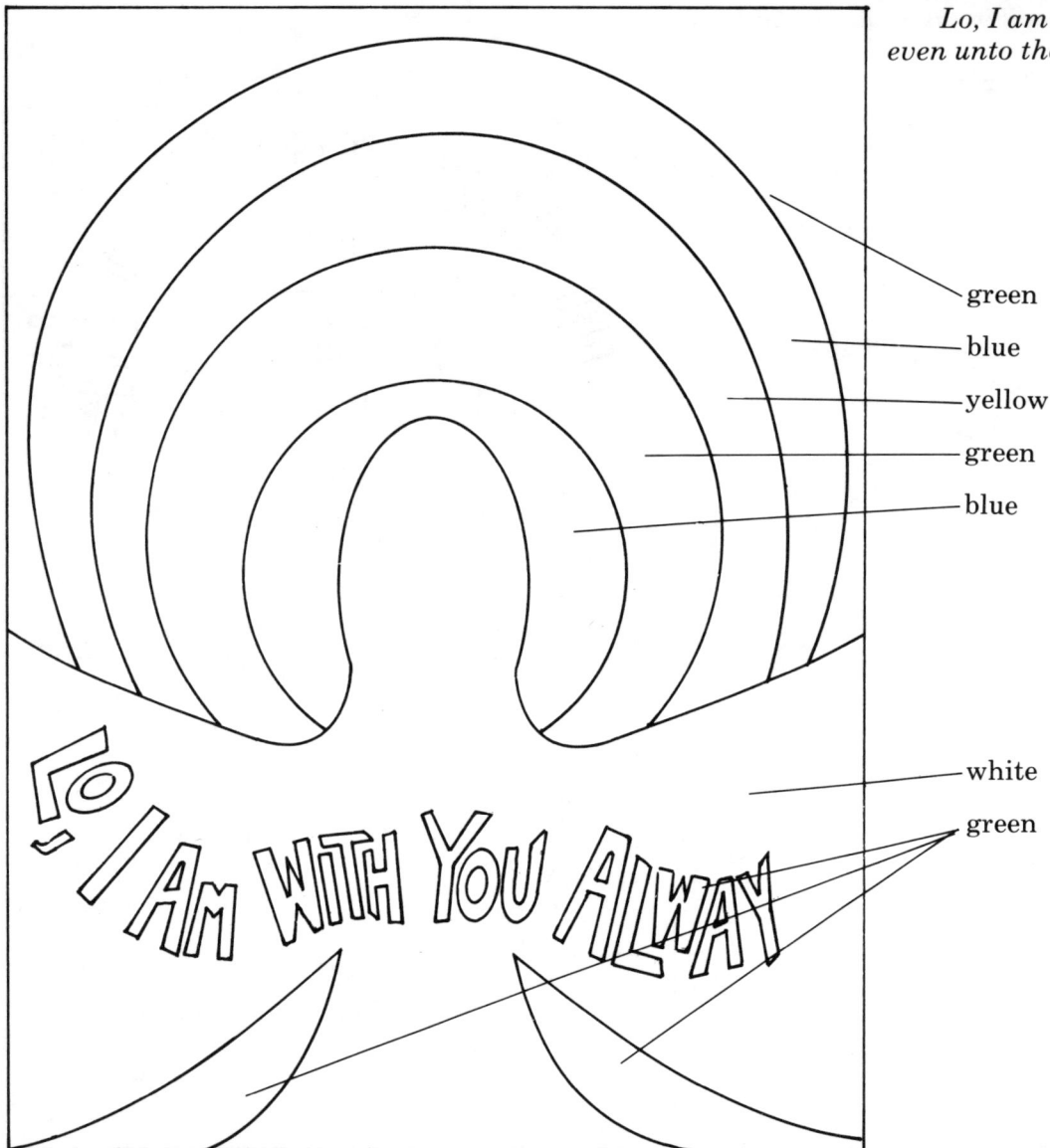

green

blue

yellow

green

blue

white

green

SUGGESTED FABRICS: Medium weight fabrics such as chino, broadcloth, or trigger in vivid colors.

In awe and silence on the Mount of Olives the disciples watched their beloved Master crown His earthly ministry by ascending to His heavenly home at the right hand of the Father's throne.

Feeling bereft of His guiding force in their lives, yet clinging to the memory of the strength He had provided, the laughter they had shared, and the knowledge He had imparted, the disciples feared that with His departure their faith would waver and their unity of purpose would be destroyed. Only His comforting words, "Lo, I am with you alway," gave them the confidence to continue. They trusted His promise to send the Spirit of truth, who would fill them with the power to persevere in their faith and go into all the world preaching the Good News.

Put on Christ

Put on the Lord Jesus Christ.

(Rom. 13:14)

green

royal blue

royal blue

gold

red

white wool

black

gold

red

Put on Christ

green

royal blue

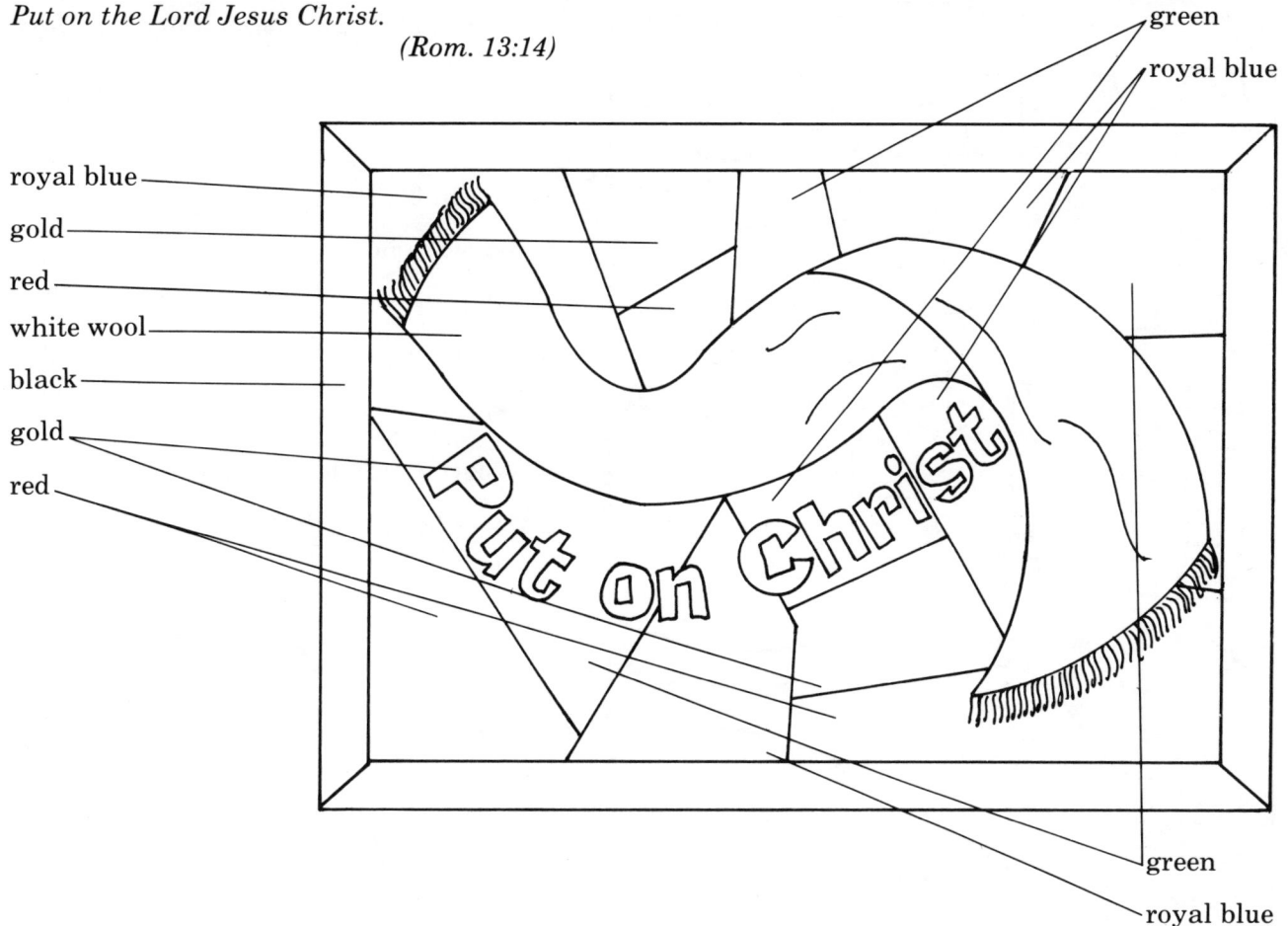

SUGGESTED FABRICS: Satin or high sheen for background (to appear as stained glass) and letters; white wool for stole (fringe as shown two inches at each end); heavy, durable fabric for black window frame. Stitch lines between each section in black for stained glass effect.

To put on something means to dress oneself in it, to make it part of one's behavior or appearance. For the Christian, putting on Christ involves discarding the old garment of self and replacing it with Christ's garment of compassion, kindness, humility, gentleness, patience, and forgiveness (Col. 3:12-13).

This metaphor is difficult to understand outside of Christianity; it must be experienced from the inside. While the rest of the world bids us march to the hollow drumbeat of self-interest, Christ calls us to play in the symphony of selfless love.

A life alive in Christ and dead to self does not suffer an identity crisis, losing the entire personality and everything held dear. On the contrary, the new person, clothed in Christ, retains his distinctive characteristics, now refined and embellished by the touch of Christ, for new purposes.

The stole in this banner reminds us that as we arise each morning and dress in the garments which clothe our bodies, we clothe our minds in Him as we "put on Christ."

ALL OCCASION

Lift ye up a banner upon the high mountain.

(Is. 13:2)

LIFT YE UP A BANNER

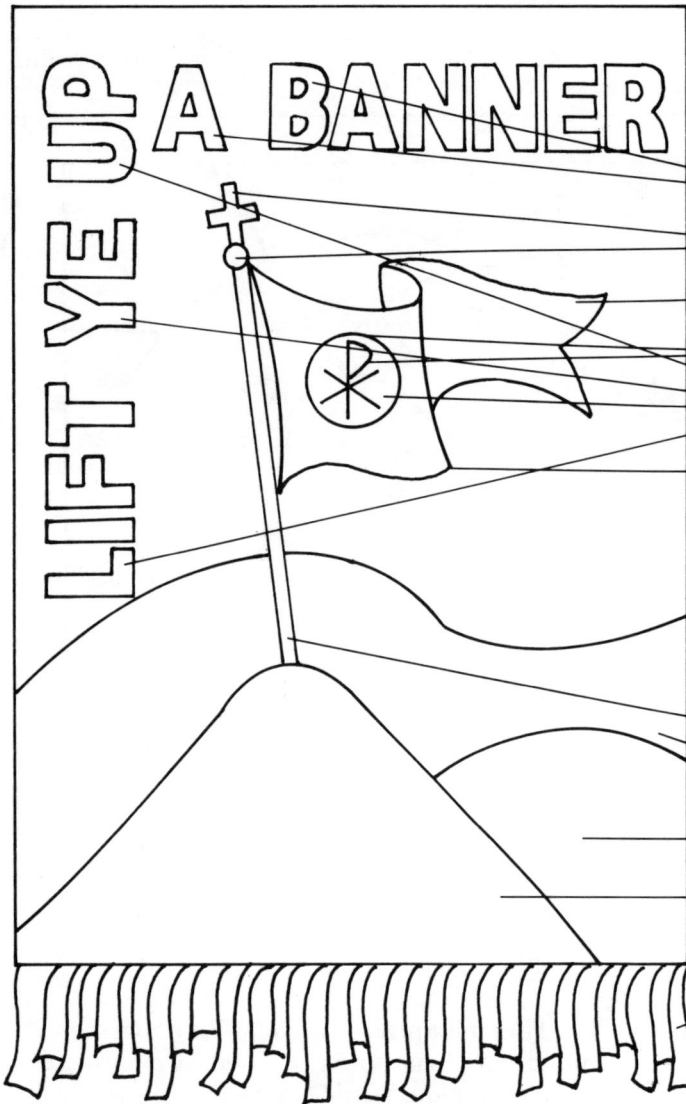

light blue

gold lamé

white

gold lamé

bright royal blue

outline stitch royal blue

dark brown

beige

light camel

camel

varying lengths (5-8″) of one-inch grosgrain ribbon in alternating colors of the banner

SUGGESTED FABRICS: Medium weight rough texture (suede cloth, no-wale corduroy, or linen-type drapery) for mountains; gold lamé for Chi Rho (enlarge) and cross with sphere; chino for banner; and medium weight trigger for everything else. Use as many banner colors as possible (with exception of gold lamé) in the streamers. Use a wooden rod to hang. (This banner would give a bolder effect in bright primary colors of red, yellow, and blue with green and white.)

Banners have been prominently lifted throughout history to signal the imminence of important events—by rulers to claim dominion, by armies as a rallying point in battle, by proponents of a cause to declare a message, by nations as symbols embodying the principles they represent, and by religions to express beliefs.

Proudly, as children of the heavenly Father, we lift His royal banner on the high mountain, acknowledging His dominion, claiming His forgiveness, waving His message of love, and rallying people of all nations to the foot of the cross where love, mercy, and grace are freely given to all who acknowledge His lordship.

The banner of the Lord bears the emblem of the Chi Rho within a circle, representing Christ in eternity, with the cross atop the standard proclaiming victory. The streamers across the bottom of the banner portray gaiety and freedom—rewards of allegiance to the heavenly King.